SOCIAL WEAPONS

The Peaceful Self Defense System Handbook

by

Chris Storey

&

Doug Casey

*Civilization began the first time
an angry person cast a word
instead of a rock*

**Sigmund Freud
Founder of psychoanalysis**

Acknowledgments

When I was a graduate student in social work at the University of Washington, I was fortunate to learn about human behavior and communication from Dr. Cornelis Bakker, who was a Professor of Psychiatry and founder of the Adult Development Program. He co-authored *No Trespassing!: Explorations in Human Territoriality.* What I learned from Dr. Bakker forms the basis for this book.

Aside from Bakker, I credit Charlotte Booth, MSW, and CEO of the Institute For Family Development in Federal Way, WA, as a co-creator of the Peaceful Self Defense System. She provided invaluable input during the writing of this book.

When I collaborated with fellow writer Doug Casey, decades of work were finally transformed into this book. If Bakker and Booth laid the foundation for Social Weapons, Casey was the mortar that solidified it.

I feel fortunate that master illustrator Steve Johannsen agreed to create the art that enhances our text.

I am thankful for the encouragement and help provided by our friends: Bob Miller, Sandy Wright, Trisha Myers, Abby DeSanchez, Carey Pivcevich, Carla Pivcevich, Gayle Watson and Jason Luedtke.

My friend Richard Helm volunteered to give the book a once over. He ended up giving it the twice over and did an amazing job improving the manuscript.

Last but not least, I'm thankful to my wife, Emi Storey, for her steadfast support, contributions to the book, and never ending inspiration.

Contents

Overview   7

Introduction to Social Weapons   10

Part I   **The 20 Social Weapons**

     1. Ridicule   24

     2. Rapid Takeover   30

     3. Gradual Takeover   41

     4. Flattery   48

     5. Helplessness   52

     6. Counterfeit Illness   57

     7. Psychoanalysis   63

     8. For Your Own Good   70

     9. Smokescreen   73

     10. Seduction   76

     11. Sex   80

12. Competence   83

13. Dress   86

14. Gifts   92

15. Over The Barrel   98

16. Guilt   106

17. Definition   113

18. Pretense   124

19. Pacifism   128

20. Withdrawal   132

Part II   Making Sense Of Conflict

21. The Territorial Behavior
     Perspective   136

22. The Concept of Territoriality   140

23. Personal and Public Territory   146

24. Territorial Behavior   164

25. Three Essential Human Needs   180

Part III   Peaceful Self Defense System Skills

26. Methods for Controlling Drama   186

27. Recognizing Irritation   188

28. Identifying the Issue of Concern   194

29. Sticking to the Issue   196

30. Bargaining   217

31. Remaining Kind and Courteous   225

32. The Warrior's Stance   230

33. Planning Strategy   235

34. Paying the Price   240

35. Handling Negative Emotions   243

36. Using Self-Reinforcement   263

37. Practicing Delayed Mastery   265

38. Signaling Defensive Intent   269

Conclusion   **276**

OVERVIEW

The weapons described in this book are not what we usually think of as weapons. They are Social Weapons comprised of words and behaviors that serve to exploit and influence people. Effective use of these manipulative devices can make it difficult for victims to control their mental and emotional composure. Most of us are unaware that Social Weapons are being used on us all the time. We have an even harder time seeing our own participation in their use. All of us tend to automatically rely on Social Weapons.

Words are loaded pistols.

Jean-Paul Sartre
French existentialist
philosopher

The Peaceful Self Defense System Handbook presents a methodology for dealing with Social Weapons and interpersonal conflict. It presents easy to learn methods for protecting social boundaries. This dynamic guide can be adapted to fit everyday conflict situations.

Recognizing our use of Social Weapons is necessary for truly being on the path to peace. This text is written to shed light on the violence behind this form of manipulative social behavior. Being able to grasp the dynamics of these weapons in action makes conflict more transparent and manageable.

In human conflict, use of Social Weapons becomes part of the problem. To be part of the solution, we must be aware of our complicity in escalating conflict. In this book we are given methods to peacefully end hostilities and abstain from battling. It is not easy to avoid antagonistic actions. Use of the Peaceful Self Defense System helps us to remain calm under attack in order to create peaceful resolutions. It provides solutions to people problems at home, work, and school, including dealing with belligerent people, getting children to take responsibility, putting an end to bullying or convincing a lazy partner to do his or her share.

Part One introduces twenty Social Weapons. A partial list includes *ridicule*, *definition*, *flattery* and *guilt*. These Social Weapons allow us to be manipulated, dominated and controlled. They are so ingrained in our social experience that most of the time we are unaware of the mechanics behind their use. All of us have experienced others trying to ruffle our feathers or inflate our egos to get their way. Identifying Social Weapons helps us quickly understand how someone is trying to take advantage of us.

Part Two presents a territorial model that provides a research based framework for understanding conflict. It defines territory as what we own or think we own, from personal property to beliefs, behaviors and ideas. Boundaries are the lines we draw to protect our perceived territory. These boundaries are continually challenged and defended with Social Weapons. We are so much a part of these territorial struggles that it is often hard to recognize what is taking place. When we look at these encounters with a territorial viewpoint it becomes easy to make sense of what others are trying to take and what we are willing to give up. Territorial awareness helps us predict and detect intrusive behavior in our forbidden zones.

Part Three describes the skills and mechanics of the Peaceful Self Defense System. This internally consistent model is designed to create harmonious relationships by encouraging mutual cooperation. Its universal approach easily generalizes to fit most adversarial social situations. With practice these methods can turn disagreements into mutual understandings.

INTRODUCTION TO SOCIAL WEAPONS

Methods of Manipulation used for
Social Survival, Domination, and Control

> *Run your finger up the gum above the eyetooth, and you will find a root out of all proportion to the size of the tooth it supports... The long root of our inconspicuous eyetooth is a nostalgic souvenir of those long-gone Miocene days when our ancestors grew natural weapons to settle discussions, as we cannot.*
>
> **Robert Ardrey**
> *African Genesis*

Our early human ancestors relied on fists, sticks, rocks, and teeth for survival. In those bygone days we were more dependent on our physical fighting prowess. The civilized weapons we use today might be less conspicuous than fangs, but they cut just as deep.

Physical conflict is still part of everyday life for too many victims of domestic and political violence. Armed conflict between nations, and among factions within nations, has occurred in some part of the globe since the beginning of recorded history. In recent decades, terrorist attacks have changed the way we operate our transportation systems and our view of safety in public places throughout the world. Inner city gang wars and battles between drug cartels kill thousands, including innocent bystanders, every year. Our prisons overflow with violent criminals. Even when physical violence is not a part of our lives, our battles are fought with violent communication.

Social Weapons are routinely employed as communication control devices to unfairly influence and manage people. Centuries of battling others with Social Weapons has made manipulative behavior seem socially acceptable. Most of us value the ability to exert control over our lives. However, the habit of using Social Weapons to handle others can get us into trouble and ruin important relationships. Reacting to the Social Weapons used on us with Social Weapons makes peace difficult to find. Striving to get our way by using Social Weapons at another's emotional expense usually escalates conflict.

> *The Golden Rule asks us to treat others as we would have them treat us. The problem is that too often we treat ourselves terribly.*
>
> **Richard Moss, MD**
> *The Mandala of Being*

Social Weapons cause anxiety, confusion, paralysis, and can leave us perplexed and easily manipulated. They cause us to feel angry, self-righteous, and vindictive. In the following story a scorpion wins his prey's trust by using several social weapons at once, including *helplessness*.

11

The Frog and The Scorpion

One day a lazy old scorpion arrived at the shore of a large pond. He wanted to be on the other side of the pond but felt it would be too hard to crawl that far. As a frog swam by, the scorpion hailed him asking, "Is there any chance I could hitch a ride across on your back?" The frog knew of the scorpion's venomous sting and was afraid. "Why should I take the chance of being stung?" asked the frog. The scorpion looked straight into the frogs eyes, smiled and softly stated, "Don't worry, frogs aren't part of my diet. I'm just too old and too worn out to try to walk around this big pond. I could really use your help." Assured, the frog swam next to the shore and allowed the scorpion to climb onto his back. When they reached the center of the pond, the scorpion punctured his host's skin with his long segmented tail, filling the frog with venom. The frog's limbs became paralyzed, he was unable to swim, and began to sink into the deep pond. Knowing they were about to die, the frog asked, "Why?" The scorpion responded, "Sorry, it's just my nature."

In this story, the scorpion got the frog's trust by using the weapons *helplessness* (too feeble) and *definition* (defined himself as being on a frog-free diet). Even though the scorpion was aware that stinging his ride (Social Weapon, *rapid takeover*) would lead to his undoing, he could not resist his instincts. It takes effort to be conscious of our own use of Social Weapons. Practice and concerted focus is necessary to curtail our use of these combative weapons. William James, the father of modern psychology, emphasized that our nature as humans has always been warlike.

>*Our ancestors have bred pugnacity into our bone and marrow, and thousands of years of peace won't breed it out of us.*
>
>**William James**
>**The Moral Equivalent of War**
>**1906 speech at Stanford University**

To decrease the influence of our inherited antagonistic nature, it makes sense to evaluate our participation in the use of Social Weapons. It is not unusual for us to stockpile these weapons for our ready use. These arsenals can be vast, composed of Social Weapons ranging from *flattery* and **ridicule** to **guilt** and **blackmail**. It is difficult to perceive, let alone admit, that we actively take part in the combative dramas that swirl around us. Most of us are unaware that we habitually manipulate others with Social Weapons.

Like the scorpion, our emotions and behavior are hard-wired to our primitive survival instincts. Our nervous systems are activated during interpersonal conflict. When we are unprepared for a verbal attack, we tend to react emotionally and often against our own best interests. Our ability to remain rational is compromised. Being able to see an attack as soon as it starts allows us to accurately evaluate the conflict and respond in a poised and peaceful manner.

It is up to us to be aware of the Social Weapons used against us. Being unaware of Social Weapons makes it difficult to see through predatory attacks.

When we operate naively, like the frog did with the scorpion, we in effect relinquish our ability to protect ourselves. Our ability to think becomes undermined when we become accomplices in our own undoing.

One of the major effects of being unable to defend against Social Weapons is the clouding of our minds with emotional venom. This reactive response usually includes hostile thoughts of retaliation or self-pity. This emotional poisoning can blind us to many of the peaceful options we can use to protect ourselves. We can help minimize our emotional reactions by understanding the lures that pull us into this type of conflict situation. By evaluating the Social Weapons that have hooked us in the past, we can better prepare more peaceful responses to future attacks.

Many of us use subtle forms of the Social Weapon *ridicule*. The use of *ridicule* to counter another's use of *ridicule* is an example of reacting using behavioral violence.

Picture an angry customer waiting in a long line. Instead of politely requesting another checker, he shouts "I'm tired of having slowpokes make me wait forever." The cashier responds by saying, "When dealing with slowpokes one should expect a long wait." This retort might seem clever, but some customers might feel ridiculed. If we want to find peaceful solutions to uncomfortable situations, it would be wise for us to keep in mind that fighting Social Weapons with Social Weapons tends to escalate conflict.

When we choose to frame an attack as an opportunity to practice the Peaceful Self Defense System, it becomes easier for us to react with kindness. Being aware of the pitfalls of Social Weapon use increases the likelihood of our going through our day without triggering counterproductive emotions.

It is common for a student of the Peaceful Self Defense System to vilify another for using Social Weapons. Critically pointing out the use of Social Weapons can make people feel under attack. If our comments make others feel uncomfortable, our remarks will be perceived as weapons. Even unintentional Social Weapon use can provoke people to take things personally and become upset.

> *Taking things personally makes you prey for predators. They can hook your attention with one little opinion, and feed you whatever poison they want. Refuse to eat poison!*
>
> **Don Miguel Ruiz**
> *The Four Agreements*

Identifying Social Weapons helps us to remain calm and focused on the mechanics of the unfolding conflict. An analytical point of view helps shield our emotional triggers and gives us an opportunity to mindfully structure a friendlier response. The Peaceful Self Defense System allows us to de-escalate conflict by being kind to ourselves and to our attackers.

Mao's Giant Hand

Dr. Ri Hui Long is a master acupuncturist practicing in Portland, Oregon. To help with my endurance running, I have a regularly scheduled appointment with him. During one of my visits, Dr. Long asked how things were going. I told him how a nasty man at the gym named Ned delivered a terrible verbal assault on me. As I related how Ned kept yelling obscenities that included unfavorable references to my mother, I began to get mad. I angrily told him I would have preferred for Ned to walk over and punch me.

Dr. Long told me that he could relate to my feelings. He told me, "My body had been tortured until it bled and my heart had been tortured until it bled. The torture of the heart and spirit is more painful and the suffering far greater."

When I asked Dr. Long to explain what happened to cause him so much pain he told me that years ago in China, Mao Tse Tung's giant hand manipulated the class struggle. Dr. Long's father had worked hard to provide a family income and so he was labeled a capitalist. This label, capitalist, turned his family into slaves. They were considered part of the same group as anti-revolutionaries and criminals. As slaves, his family suffered from material poverty, but they even suffered more from the systematic brainwashing.

Dr. Long told me how his assigned political instructor demanded that he betray himself and his family. He constantly had to report any unacceptable thoughts that crossed his mind. He had to confess doing wrong and constantly criticize himself. Even worse, he had to condemn his family, grandfather, and ancestors. When he denounced his family he felt like his heart was bleeding. Eventually his heart felt numb. Finally, he almost believed that his family committed the sins he reported. Dr. Long explained that this experience was powerful enough to distort his personality. It stripped away his dignity, made him feel that he had been born a criminal, and threw him into a state of dark desperation. He said, "Even when the sun shone in through the cleft of the window, I never cheered for a new day as I faced another forced atonement."

Studies suggest that verbal abuse can be even more emotionally destructive than a beating.

Richard Conniff
The Ape In The Corner Office

Dr. Long then inserted an acupuncture needle into the top of my head. I asked him what it was for. He told me that it was so I wouldn't have to think for a while about the horrible ways some people treat others.

After the acupuncture treatment, thirty-six hours went by before I thought again about Ned's verbal attack. I thought back to how I had handled the entire onslaught at the gym. I had done nothing to embarrass myself. But after leaving the situation, I had lost control of my thoughts and begun to take the incident personally. I became angry and self-righteous and things began to unravel. I instinctively felt that I had every right to be filled with hate, and automatically started consuming emotional poison. Later, Dr. Long's story helped free me from this reactive state and put an end to my self-pity.

Contrasting my trivial encounter to Dr. Long's story, I was able to see how my overly dramatic thoughts had thrown me into a situation where extrication had become very difficult. My emotions were no longer triggered when I reviewed the incident. I was collected enough to see that my ordeal was minor compared to the severity of Dr. Long's nightmarish childhood. I reflected on the relative insignificance of my experience. Finally, I was able to change my perspective so I was no longer emotionally bound to Ned's actions.

Once I was able to look inward from a detached and more aware point of view, I realized I had been participating in a self-perpetuating melodrama. I saw how I had been emotionally triggered by Social Weapons and how I was unconsciously rubbing salt into my emotional wounds. Before hearing Dr. Long's story, it was difficult for me to be aware of my own habitual thought patterns. Like a panicked fly, the more I struggled with my emotional webs the more I became entangled.

We can decrease our chances of becoming entwined in webs of emotions by making a habit of monitoring and modifying our reactionary thoughts. The onset of emotions can be used in a positive way. When our emotions start to awaken, we can let them warn us of impending conflict. Emotions can be used as a reminder to move our thoughts to the mechanics of the attack. By focusing on the Social Weapons being used, we are given the clarity needed to avoid becoming ensnared in an emotional panic.

No man can think clearly
when his fists are clenched.

George Jean Nathan
American Writer

It is not unusual for us to have to deal with a tyrannical boss, intolerant spouse, incorrigible teenager, or a bullying colleague. When under fire, our mental stability is enhanced if we are weapon-aware and confident. Mental clarity and emotional control are paramount in improving our ability to effectively respond to a variety of behavioral attacks.

Awareness of Social Weapons is what gives us the freedom to avoid becoming easy targets. When we are unaware of the Social Weapons we use on ourselves, we narrow our understanding and become subject to losing emotional control.

Sanford and Son

Former President Bill Clinton presented Norman Lear with a 1999 National Medal of Arts award, saying, "Lear has held up a mirror to American society and changed the way we look at it." Lear's 1972 NBC television program *Sanford and Son* chronicled the adventures of Fred G. Sanford, a cantankerous junkyard owner living with his grown son, Lamont.

In order to get his way with Lamont, Fred would grasp his chest, look upwards towards heaven and call to his departed wife, "Elizabeth, this is the big one, here I come." Fred exaggerated his heart condition to manipulate Lamont. By using the Social Weapon *counterfeit illness*, Fred tried to get Lamont to fall prey to the Social Weapon *guilt.* Fred's goal was to control Lamont by faking a heart attack.

In attempts to disarm his overbearing sister-in-law Esther, Fred would routinely use the Social Weapon *ridicule* to attack and insult her. Fred unrelentingly taunted Esther by comparing her to monsters like King Kong and Godzilla. She usually would appear unfazed and would readily mount her own vicious verbal attacks. When Fred used Social Weapons on Esther, it only served to beckon more conflict as Esther invariably returned fire. This television program was a dramatization of how Social Weapons are constantly backfiring as a consequence of their use.

> *War is like unto fire; those who will not put aside weapons are themselves consumed by them.*
>
> **Sun Tzu**
> *The Art of War*

Social Weapons cause anxiety, confusion, paralysis, and leave us perplexed and easily manipulated. They also cause us to feel angry, self-righteous, and vindictive. Even when we are feeling rejuvenated and ready for action, we are susceptible to manipulative attacks.

Twenty Social Weapons

The next section presents the mechanics of twenty Social Weapons that are habitually used to control people. Being able to grasp how the following Social Weapons work is the starting point for creating peace out of conflict. The twenty Social Weapons are:

1. Ridicule
2. Rapid Takeover
3. Gradual Takeover
4. Flattery
5. Helplessness
6. Counterfeit Illness
7. Psychoanalysis
8. For Your Own Good
9. Smoke Screen
10. Seduction
11. Sex
12. Competence
13. Dress
14. Gifts
15. Over The Barrel
16. Guilt
17. Definition
18. Pretense
19. Pacifism
20. Withdrawal

The upcoming section on Social Weapons is only a snapshot of how they are used to coerce us during human conflict. In the real world, these weapons continue to surprise us all. They are often hidden in accepted social behavior and used in dramatic combinations seemingly impossible to track.

Being surprised by an angry person using Social Weapons can be as overwhelming as finding oneself face to face with a home intruder. When under social attack, our chances of remaining calm are increased when we are able to anticipate and/or understand the Social Weapons being used against us. By learning about the dynamics of Social Weapons, we can improve our ability to see through the stealth of most behavioral assaults.

PART ONE

THE 20 SOCIAL WEAPONS

Chapter 1

RIDICULE

The Social Weapon *ridicule* is often difficult to defend against because of the overwhelming emotional charge it triggers. *Ridicule* attacks our most vulnerable target, our ego. It insults us, mocks us, humiliates us and creates laughter for others at our expense.

The Three Finger Glove

Luke* worked as a salesman at a glove factory. The owner and operator of the factory was a lady named Kim who micromanaged everyone and everything at her business. She was so much "the boss" that she felt entitled to step on the toes of all her employees. She criticized and berated everyone around her. Kim's sister also worked at the factory and was her constant companion. Kim enjoyed making her sister laugh at her outrageous put-downs. The attrition that took place at the company was enormous. Workers regularly called in

---

* In the interest of protecting privacy, most names are not real.

24

sick to look for new jobs because they dreaded being ridiculed by Kim.

Luke was landing contracts at a record pace. The problem was that Kim insisted on meeting all new clients. During client meetings Kim would habitually gossip with her sister. The targets were Luke and the other employees. She would say, "They're lucky I hired them. If I don't stay on top of them they're likely to start selling gloves with only three fingers. No one but me would put up with them." Many of the clients found her so abrasive that they terminated their accounts. Luke along with the rest of the sales staff grew tired of Kim's public lambasting and all quit at the same time.

Fried Hair

A young student named Monica worked at the University Bookstore. She just had her hair done and was feeling pretty good about herself. Early during the morning shift her older coworker Barbara looked at Monica with disgust and said, "Your hair looks really fried, hope you asked for your money back." Monica pretended that she didn't hear the insult and continued working. A little later that morning Barbara told Monica, "I was just kidding earlier, actually your hair is kind of cute." "Oh, thanks," Monica replied. Barbara then said, "But, if the hair dresser had a conscience, she wouldn't have taken your money!" Monica then responded by saying, "You are so not with it! I'm more concerned with what the guys will think of my new look." Barbara rolled her eyes and said, "Yeah, like the bride of Frankenstein look!" Monica shook her head in disbelief and walked away mumbling, "What a bitch! Now I know why everyone hates you."

Monica reacted to being ridiculed by leveling an insult of her own. Typically this tit for tat behavior serves only to elevate tension and hateful feelings.

Saddam's Reaction

In 1990, the dictator of Iraq, Saddam Hussein, was at the pinnacle of his power. He commanded one of the largest standing armies in the world. Saddam ordered his generals to attack the country of Kuwait. That action precipitated the warfare that eventually led to Saddam's demise.

Saddam's actions brought him unfavorable attention that eventually led to his being captured, interrogated and executed. George Piro of the FBI was assigned to interview the deposed dictator and nonviolently extract information from him prior to his trial.

Piro started interviewing Saddam not long after he was pulled from his underground hiding place. These interviews took place daily for a period of seven months. Piro got the answers to why Saddam attacked Kuwait. He was able to understand what motivated many of Saddam's other historic actions. There were many theories as to why Saddam invaded Kuwait, but Piro learned for the first time that the brutal invasion was triggered by a personal insult.

According to Saddam, he had sent his foreign minister to Kuwait to try to resolve some oil and loan issues. The Emir Sheikh Jabr al-Sabah of Kuwait told the foreign minister of Iraq that he "Would not stop doing what he was doing until he turned every Iraqi woman into a ten dollar prostitute." Piro said, "That sealed it for Saddam to invade Kuwait. He wanted to punish Emir Jabr al-Sabah for saying that."

If they want peace, nations should avoid the pinpricks that precede cannon-shots.

Napoleon Bonaparte

The Emir's insulting use of ***ridicule*** is an example of a pinprick that created catastrophic consequences. The United States and the United Nations used military force to liberate Kuwait. It has become second nature for most of us to react to Social Weapons by using Social Weapons. We often take the point of view that we are responding appropriately because we believe we are in the right. When we think in terms of being right, we tend to let our intended end justify the means to get there. The problem is that when we rely on Social Weapons, the end can become destructive and unpredictable.

A major disadvantage of using weaponry when we speak is that its use almost invariably creates hostility

27

in others. We have unconsciously learned to depend on Social Weapons because they seem to work with little effort. This reliance on Social Weapons can have oppressive effects on our families, friends, adversaries and us. Broadening our choices to include Peaceful Self Defense System strategies can keep us from clobbering or getting clobbered.

When the only tool you own is a hammer, every problem begins to resemble a nail.

Abraham Harold Maslow
Father of Humanistic Psychology

All In The Family

In the 1970's Norman Lear had another highly successful sitcom called *All In The Family.* Carroll O'Connor was cast as Archie Bunker, an aggressively prejudiced blue-collar worker. Archie would use the Social Weapon *ridicule* as he referred to his wife Edith as 'Ding Bat' and his son-in-law Michael as 'Meat Head'. His crude use of Social Weapons to bully others was easy for viewers to see. To survive life with Archie, his family members would typically team up against him with Social Weapons that further intensified the conflict. Archie would often tell Edith, "Go stifle yourself." Edith would be told to stifle herself again and again until finally in one episode she turned to Archie and unexpectedly said in her shrill voice, "No Archie, you stifle yourself!"

This ramping up of Social Weapon use would create behavioral lures that routinely resulted in the characters experiencing emotional meltdowns. Just as in this comedy, when people on both sides of a dispute choose to use Social Weapons, the aftermath is usually counterproductive for all participants.

When confronted with insults, an understanding of the psychology behind *ridicule* can help curtail our tendency to be reactive. Identifying *ridicule* as a manipulative tool makes it easier for us to remain calm.

Chapter 2

RAPID TAKEOVER

With ***rapid takeover***, the aggressor instantly assumes control over another's territory. That territory can be possessions, power, ideas, influence, dignity, confidence or attention. This seizing of property is accomplished before it can be stopped. It is very difficult to protect what has already been lost. The defender is put in a position where he has to mount a counterattack, find another way to recoup his loses, or just give up. Counterattacking can be costly and often requires a great deal of energy.

> *All is unceasing and rigorous competition in nature; the desire to make off with the substance of others is the foremost passion nature has bred into us.*
>
> **Marquis de Sade**
> **French Novelist**

Walled Off

During a Peaceful Self Defense System workshop a participant related an unbelievable story that occurred at his workplace. Bradley, the senior sales manager, was well liked by his colleagues. He was fond of the lake view his office afforded. After a very successful sales campaign Bradley took a two week vacation to New Zealand.

While Bradley was gone, his best friend Bob convinced the entire office to participate in a practical joke. Bob hired a remodeler to take out Bradley's office door and extend the wall over the entrance. It was dry walled and painted to look like his office never existed. A large framed photo of the lake was hung at the location of the former doorway.

When Bradley returned from his trip, he felt a little jet-lagged but eager to see what new challenges might have come up at work. When he walked down the hall to his office, no one was greeting him. His co-workers acted as if he were invisible. He started to look very perplexed as he ran his fingers along the wall as he futilely searched for his office door. Finally his staff burst into laughter, took turns hugging him, shaking his hand and welcoming him back. This is an example of the Social Weapon *rapid takeover* briefly removing someone's identification and personal territory.

Resumé Heist

Fredrick worked at an advertising company as an entry level office worker. Paul was one of Fredrick's co-workers. Paul had a strong dislike for Fredrick. They were both vying for the same supervisory position. Frederick had been working on his resume for several long nights and was well prepared for his promotion interview. His interview was about to take place in less than fifteen minutes. Paul had just finished his interview and was heading out for lunch when he noticed Fredrick's resumé folder. It was on Fredrick's desk with no one else nearby. Paul instantly slipped the folder into his briefcase and left the office.

During the resumé heist, Frederick was in the restroom tidying himself up for his interview. When he returned to his cubicle he looked around and could not find the folder that contained his resumé and other support material needed for his interview. He even searched the hallway and the restroom trash. At two minutes before the interview, Fredrick had worked himself into a major state of panic. Even though he was almost sure he had taken his folder into the office building, he ran out to his car at the far end of the parking lot in a last ditch attempt to recover his paperwork. Fredrick was sweating and looking quite unkempt as he entered the interview room.

As in the above example, stealing is one form of the Social Weapon *rapid takeover*. Paul not only took Fredrick's possession, he stole Fredrick's composure and confidence, lowering his probability of a successful interview.

The Manager's New Idea

It is not unusual for people at work to lay claim to their coworkers' ideas. Shelley, one of my students, related to me that she was a victim of such a theft. Shelley told her manager about a new idea she had for cutting costs at work. The manager told her that she must have been reading his mind and that he had already told his boss the exact same idea. The manager then hurried to the boss' office to present his new idea. The manager beamed with pride after his presentation. To the manager's surprise, his boss was frowning. Shelly had actually mentioned her idea to the boss <u>before</u> she told her manager, when passing the boss in the hall. The boss had told Shelley to run the idea past her manager so he would have the opportunity to implement it.

Shelley was lucky to avoid her manager's attempted ***rapid takeover*** of her idea. If Shelley had told her unscrupulous manager about the idea first, she would have had very little chance of reclaiming her idea once it was taken.

Queen of The Road

My mother was an accomplished ***rapid takeover*** artist. Divorced and having to support the family she worked six days a week as an office manager in Los Angeles. Mom was overworked, underpaid and always in a big hurry. When getting in the car to go somewhere the pace really picked up. Often before I had a chance to fully close the car door, Mom would slam her foot on the gas pedal. Her tires would typically be burning rubber as we sped up the street. My mother's race against time would meet various obstacles like the dreaded stop sign.

Venice Boulevard was one block from our old home on Kingsley Drive. During my years attending elementary school the traffic from Venice Boulevard seemed never ending. The continuous stream of vehicles during the morning rush hour made it almost impossible for anyone trying to make a left turn from Kingsley Drive. Mom was in too much of a hurry to get me to school before work to wait at the stop sign. The moment Mom's car came to a stop at this intersection, I was assigned to leap out of the car door and run to the left side of Kingsley Drive. My task was to quickly step into the crosswalk in front of the oncoming traffic that traveled on Venice Boulevard.

The oncoming cars were forced to stop to avoid hitting me as I was in the crosswalk and had the right of way. One of my tricks was to step out onto the street while appearing to be unconscious of the cars traveling in my direction. Usually after dodging an initial car or two, I would get the rest of the cars to stop as I assumed control of the crosswalk. My mom would track me in a parallel course as she began to drive across Venice Boulevard. As soon as I was almost to the end of the crosswalk, she would hurriedly make a left turn behind my heels and briefly stop. I would then scurry back to the car and brace for the lunge forward as she punched the gas pedal. Typically we would burst out laughing after once again successfully seizing possession of the road.

My mother and I used the Social Weapon *rapid takeover* to regularly control that intersection. After years of practice I became a skilled accomplice to mom's acquisition of this desired territory.

The Martians Are Coming

Cornelis Bakker, M.D., professor of psychiatry at the University of Washington, held a weekly staff meeting and encouraged participation from all the instructors, including Charlotte and me. We had just returned from a course about healing and enlightenment. Dr. Bakker enthusiastically opened the meeting saying he wanted to hear all about our experience. Charlotte and I were having a wonderful time presenting the magical things we had learned. The other members of the staff were asking positive questions and seemed to consider the topic worthy of discussion. After about thirty minutes, which was half way through the meeting, things began to get very strange for the two of us. Dr. Bakker slowly asked, "What if aliens came down from

outer space and listened to what we are talking about? I don't think they would understand about healing presented this way. If these aliens were from Mars we shouldn't be talking about this at all." Dr. Bakker gazed up, raised his arm and pointed toward the ceiling, as though he saw a flying saucer about to land. He finished his comments with a smirk and a roll of his eyes.

Following Dr. Bakker's statements, the staff became contrary and argued with everything we talked about for the remainder of the meeting. The negativity was unexpected and made it difficult for us to think clearly. We were no longer having a wonderful time. Near the end of the staff meeting, Dr. Bakker laughed and let us off the hook by stating that he was actually quite open to the merits of our presentation.

Dr. Bakker went on to explain that his actions were an experiment. He wanted to see if putting a negative spin on the topic at the halfway point would create ongoing resistance for Charlotte and me. His use of *rapid takeover* worked like magic, turning the entire staff against us. He demonstrated how easy it was to undermine the validity of what was being shared. It was a lesson to the staff on how quickly a person of authority can change a collective point of view. Everything he said about Martians was nonsense and simply a vehicle to seize control.

The Social Weapon *rapid takeover* can be as obvious as my jumping out in front of traffic to stop cars for my mom. *Rapid takeover* can also be used in a subtle way. Dr. Bakker's sideshow skillfully snatched control of the meeting and changed everyone's attitude.

Rapid takeover is used on us all the time. Our condo has assigned parking spaces and more often than not we find our neighbor's friend parked in our reserved space. When our parking space is being occupied by someone else's car, some of our personal territory has been taken from us.

During private conversations someone might interrupt us and take away our ability to continue discussing something very important to us. Our privacy and our time would be stolen through the unwanted and possibly unintended use of *rapid takeover*.

Rapid takeover can upset us when someone arrives two hours late for an important meeting without calling to warn us. When a spouse is very late for a special dinner, the one doing the cooking often feels the emotional effects of this Social Weapon. Showing up too early is another form of *rapid takeover* that can be just as bothersome. For instance, this could be when a guest arrives during last minute preparations for a party.

Laurence Gonzales, in his bestselling book *Deep Survival*, explained how some people survive potentially disastrous encounters with nature. He emphasizes that the people who live through extreme survival situations do so by being in the here and now. Being present in the moment is not limited to surviving in nature's wilderness. This focusing on what is currently happening can keep us mentally collected as everyday events unfold before us.

Instant recognition of *rapid takeover* can keep us from becoming disturbed and victimized. Anytime we encounter *rapid takeover* we have the option to follow Gonzales' first rule of life. By being present in the now, we improve our ability to evaluate our circumstances and options. This is because we have less chance of being distracted and detoured by our own emotional reactivity. Having a clear view of a situation increases our chances for finding a suitable response.

When we allow our minds to be lost in the past or future, we relinquish options for survival. For instance, if our thoughts are elsewhere when someone picks our pocket, we become victims of our unawareness. *Rapid takeover* is most successfully employed on us when our minds are elsewhere.

> *Being lost, then, is not a location; it is a transformation. It is a failure of the mind.*
>
> **Laurence Gonzales**
> *Deep Survival*

Even when we are well trained in the Peaceful Self Defense System, it is difficult to undo what has already happened. *Rapid takeover* can beat us to the punch when we step into the ring of life with our eyes closed. When personal territory is snatched from us, it can be difficult to avoid becoming upset. Strong emotions like anger can cause our minds to overlook peaceful solutions.

I Just Have A Few Items

Sharon was shopping at the community supermarket and had been waiting in the checkout line for a long time. She was the next customer to be served when a tall woman with a few items walked to the front of the line and put her items down on the conveyer belt. The woman who cut in line was well dressed and oozed with confidence. Her authoritative presence instantly demanded the attention of all those around her. Sharon listened in disbelief as this woman ignored the people waiting in line, faced the cashier, smiled and sweetly said, "I just have a few items."

Sharon mustered her will and with a cracking voice complained to the cashier that this woman had just cut in front of her. The cashier ignored Sharon, quickly ran the woman's items and took her money. After she departed, the rest of the people in line suddenly awoke to what had just happened. The once sleepy line of shoppers came to life as everyone began to complain about the nerve of the woman who just cut in line.

After Sharon left the store, she stayed mad for the rest of the day and yelled at her kids.

40

Chapter 3

GRADUAL TAKEOVER

Gradual takeover is a Social Weapon that is used to take over another's territory in small stages. This form of intrusion is carried out bit-by-bit or step-by-step, taking a little at a time.

> *More often territory is not*
> *taken in one massive action,*
> *but piecemeal.*
>
> **Cornelis B. Bakker, M.D.**
> **Marianne Bakker-Rabdau**
> *No Trespassing!: Explorations*
> *in Human Territoriality*

Slow Bite and Blow

The late Dr. Maya Angelou is known for her poems and other works that have enlightened others to the human condition. During one of her appearances on the Oprah Winfrey Show, she discussed a sly African animal's feeding behavior. When this creature is hungry it slowly consumes a portion of live flesh without being detected. This bite after bite exploitation is accomplished by relying on its prey's lack of presence. The predator just nibbles on its sleeping or preoccupied victims until a reaction is detected. When the prey begins to stir, the predator blows air on the bite to soothe any discomfort. When the victim's attention drifts away from the wound the exploitation resumes. The predator can continue feasting by taking small bites, and by continually soothing its victim's wounds.

Just as it is done in the rest of the Animal Kingdom, humans are constantly taking small bites out of one another.

Irma Shares a Room

Climbing a ladder to get into her attic proved dangerous for eighty-year-old Irma. When Irma reached the top rung of the attic ladder her foot slipped and she fell all the way down to the floor. She landed on her sacrum and broke her pelvis. Irma's accident precipitated weeks of rehab therapy at a nursing home.

For the first three weeks Irma was alone in a two-person room. At the beginning of the fourth week an eighty-two year old woman named Mabel was moved in. Mabel had a broken hip and was in alcohol withdrawal. When Mabel's son visited, he grabbed the television remote from Irma's bedstead and made it available to Mabel. The next day, the son changed the angle of the television so his mother could easily see it. Irma who had arthritis in her neck could not turn her head far enough to see the television screen. Later that week, Mabel's son turned the television to an over-the-top fire and brimstone religious channel and then left for home. Irma, a devout Catholic, did not like what she was hearing and was especially upset that the volume was turned up unbearably high.

After a few hours a nurse came in and turned off the television and Irma managed to fall asleep. When Irma awoke she needed to use her bedpan. The bedpan was missing and the curtain was now drawn around Mabel's bed. After a few minutes the curtain was pulled back and Mabel's daughter Violet stepped out with the bedpan. She went into the bathroom and emptied the bedpan. Irma asked if she had happened to take her bedpan. Violet said she was very sorry for taking the pan, but her mother had to use it. Violet placed the bedpan on the side table next to her mother. Irma reached for the telephone to call and get another bedpan, but found it too was missing. Before Irma could say anything Violet had pulled the curtain closed again around her mother's bed and turned the television back on and up a bit louder than before.

Within a few days Mabel's family had, bit-by-bit, taken control of the room. The family's point of view was fixed solely on their mother's behalf with no regard as to how their actions affected Irma. Because Irma, her family, and the health care providers inadequately responded to each step of the *gradual takeover*, Mabel's family turned the room into her own dominion.

Werner's Property Line

My friend Werner often complained about his neighbor, who shared a backyard property line with Werner's place. Each year, when planting his spring garden, the neighbor took over more of Werner's backyard. It began with about a one-foot intrusion. After five years the neighbor had established his garden on approximately six hundred square feet of Werner's backyard.

One day Werner was particularly exasperated with his situation and he asked me what I would do if I were in his shoes. I asked, "Have you considered putting up a fence?" Werner responded, "Well, I don't want to do anything that might create bad feelings." I then said, "If you put it up during the winter you might avoid upsetting your neighbor. Also, you need to consider the bad feelings that are festering inside yourself! By setting clear boundaries with a fence, things should mellow out before you know it." Werner realized he had failed to act decisively to counter the intrusion.

Whiner's Disease

The Social Weapon *gradual takeover* can come in the form of constant whining. Whiners who use this Social Weapon manipulate us by wearing us down with their misery.

Melody grew up whining about any problem that confronted her. Actually she would invent problems, make mountains out of mole hills, and complain constantly. She created a fine art of using her self-imposed misery to avoid doing anything she might consider as work. If her parents gave her a task to do, it was predictable that she would complain about having to do it. She would react with a pained nasal whine, "Do I have to?" Sometimes she would grumble, "You're so mean, making me take out the trash when it's so cold out!" Or she would snivel, "You guys are something else, making me slave when it's hot out!" She would weep and fret about how some of her friends had maid service at their homes. Any inconvenience or chore became a major battle. Usually Melody's parents would just end up doing the task for Melody rather than having to endure her peevishness.

The more success Melody experienced with whining the more she was inclined to whine. The other whiners at school would join Melody in whining sessions that made this behavior seem like the norm to her. Most of Melody's fellow whiners did not view their own complaining as whining and would bad mouth Melody's incessant whining behind her back.

After Melody married and left home several things happened. Her parents were relieved. Her husband was sorry he married her. Her boss regretted having hired her. Upbeat people would avoid her like the plague. She often whined to her psychiatrist about how he was the only one who would listen to her.

Whining is a classic form of **gradual takeover**. This Social Weapon begins as slightly tolerable but the cumulative effects ends up overwhelming its victims. Melody's initial use of this Social Weapon was to get out of doing chores. She habitually wore down her parents and later her husband with her whining to such an extent that they could no longer stand being around her. Before their divorce, her husband would often say, "Honey, you are not happy unless you are unhappy."

When we continue whining we are using the Social Weapon *gradual takeover*. The victim is either trapped in misery, learns to ignore us, or runs. This irritating form of *gradual takeover* can harden the listener's heart and cause the weapon user to become increasingly isolated and disliked.

Chapter 4

FLATTERY

Flattery is the Social Weapon that relies on the victim being susceptible to ego stroking. It is common to unknowingly become enticed by the seductive trap of praise. Our ability to recognize *flattery* being used as a Social Weapon is diminished by our craving for compliments. When oblivious of others' hidden agendas, *flattery* can leave our egos feeling gratified, overly confident, and an easy target for manipulation. Sometimes *flattery* is cloaked in a simple request for advice or information. When skillfully carried out, this form of pumping up victims can make them focus on their superiority and be less aware that they are in the process of being had.

Richard Conniff's book, *The Ape In The Corner Office*, touched on the topic of manipulating with *flattery*. Mr. Conniff writes, "Despite what everybody says about hating *flattery*, it is an essential tool for subordinates." He implies that underlings at the workplace sometimes use stealth tactics to get ahead. He remarks, "...this is the shrewd subordinate who will make his flattering remarks to a well-situated third party, confident that they will promptly be passed along to the boss."

The word flattery itself derives from a French
word meaning to stroke or caress.
Richard Conniff
The Ape In The Corner Office

You're So Good

Sally is a licensed massage therapist. During her bodywork sessions, some of her clients tend to ramp up the *flattery* meter. Sally reports, "When a client raves about how great I am at giving massages, I always seem to end up giving them extra time. The recovery time I scheduled for myself between appointments tends to disappear in direct relationship to the increase in compliments."

Sally is very good at helping people feel physically and mentally better. By day's end she is often exhausted and has nothing left to give. Usually after a day's work the Social Weapon *flattery* has been a big factor in the emptying of her energy reserves.

Compliments used as *flattery* can make us feel warm and fuzzy. It is easier for others to manipulate us when we are unaware that our egos are getting stroked. Buying into *flattery* can blind us from seeing important manipulative clues as we become mentally impaired with inflated feelings of pride. When lured into the blinders of ego gratification, we are less likely to suspect that there are ulterior motives involved.

Used Again

Rod was a hard working bodybuilder and not much of a lady's man. The guys at our gym were amused when Rod was reeled in to rescuing a woman who needed someone with muscle to help her move. Margie used *flattery* in combination with the weapons *helplessness* and *seduction* to get Rod to do her bidding. She complimented his physique. By charming Rod's ego, she was able to get him to play the role of a hero. Margie manipulated Rod by getting him to feel sorry for her and by making him think that she was attracted to him on a more personal level.

This charmer managed her relationship with Rod so the manipulation would remain one sided. The routine was painful to watch. Anytime Margie needed manual labor, she would come on strong with her body language and eye contact while seductively saying something like, "Oh, Rod you are sure lookin' good! I could use a man with a body like yours." In the end, Rod was charmed, used, and discarded.

The Social Weapon *flattery* is often used with the intent to gain a desired outcome. Cornelis Bakker, MD often said, "Intentions don't count!" When we believe we are being complimented with good intentions it is easy to accept well placed praise. It does not matter if the users of praise are sincere or not with their compliments. What matters is how we perceive praise.

If we feel alarmed by someone's use of *flattery*, it is sensible to ask, "Is that person trying to manipulate me?"

Chapter 5

HELPLESSNESS

Helplessness is the appearance of being incapable, needy, or incompetent. People often act as if they can't do something hoping someone else will do the task for them.

What Are You Doing?

When attending undergraduate school, I lived in a small apartment in Seal Beach, California. My mother lived close by and would sometimes stop by to see me. During one of her visits she observed my girlfriend, Kathy, slowly and carefully ironing one of my shirts and asked, "What are you doing?" Kathy replied, "I'm ironing his clothes."   My mother inquired incredulously, "Why isn't he ironing them?"   Kathy responded, "Oh! He isn't very good at it, so I often stop by and give him a hand." My mother replied, "Not very good at it?!?" He had to do all his ironing growing up, he's not only good at it, but he is fast. Let's go for a walk and let Chris do his own ironing!"

I had fabricated the story that I was helpless when it came to ironing. The truth was, I hated ironing and used *helplessness* to manipulate someone into doing it for me. After my mom busted me, Kathy never ironed for me again.

Helplessness is a powerful Social Weapon that is used for personal gain or to avoid unwanted challenges. One problem with using this weapon is that the user's actual capabilities must remain hidden. Once we decide to play the role of helpless or incompetent, others begin to keep a wary eye on us. This 'weapon' can get us stuck in a role of lying to those around us. We can become so habituated to our story that we end up believing it and thus limited by our own lies.

The Little Blind Dog

"Stop!" screamed Clyde as he darted out into the busy street waving his massive arms. He had seen a feeble little dog dangerously close to being run over by speeding cars. He grabbed the dog and leapt for the sidewalk barely avoiding being hit by traffic. As he checked to see if the dog was okay he noticed that its eyes appeared to be blinded by white coatings. Clyde assumed they were cataracts. In search for the dog's owner, he then proceeded to canvas what he discovered to be an ethnic Russian neighborhood.

The residents in this community appeared uneasy of outsiders entering their domain. Clyde, being a giant of a man, cut an imposing image that made people cautious of him. He moved from house to house asking, "Hi, have you ever seen this dog before?" The usual response was, "I'm Russian, don't speak English." They appeared to be in the habit of feigning an inability to converse in English in order to keep from getting involved with questionable strangers.

Clyde politely pressed the conversation while emphasizing his concern for the dog. This persistent approach made it possible for him to keep from being easily dismissed. It became obvious that he was going to remain in their neighborhood until the little pooch was returned to his owners. Most of the locals discontinued their use of the Social Weapon *helplessness* once they realized how intent Clyde was in finding the dog's owners. Many of the people he encountered in this community actually ended up speaking fairly fluent English.

Clyde continued to ignore any overtures of *helplessness* and his perseverance ended up saving the day for the lost dog. Eventually word got out to the dog's owner and it was returned home. The little creature was wagging its tail as it literally shot into the air and landed into its master's outstretched arms.

Following Orders

During the Nuremberg International War Trials, German Nazi SS Lt. Colonel Adolph Eichmann defended his crimes against humanity, which included his participation in organizing the Holocaust, by testifying that he and his fellow officers were merely following orders. In order to avoid committing treason, these soldiers justified their crimes by claiming that the bureaucratic rules left them no other option but rigid compliance. Government directives could not be disobeyed and a soldier had no choice but to follow commands. This justification only worked as long as the Nazis were in power. Following the War Trials, Eichmann was found guilty and executed.

The institutionalized lack of options is an effective way to preserve obedience. Sub-ordinates are given a directive of *helplessness* in order to assure their compliance to mandates. Bureaucrats can take *helplessness* and turn it into an art form. Many financial companies use *helplessness* as part of a systematic strategy to increase their profits. Those trying to operate outside their rules usually find a seemingly robot-like person reiterating company policy while explaining that they are unable to meet out-of-bounds requests. The customer service representative might say, "I'm sorry, I would like to help you, but our regulations prohibit me from waiving these charges." Using the Social Weapon *helplessness* by passing the blame to policy makers has become an accepted customer service mode of operation. This form of *helplessness* is called *bureaucratic helplessness*.

Chapter 6

COUNTERFEIT ILLNESS

A close cousin to *helplessness* is the Social Weapon *counterfeit illness*. It is regularly used when a person plays the role of being more of an invalid than he or she actually is. The use of *counterfeit illness* to get what one wants is most effective when others are unable to discern the extent of the exaggeration.

> *Counterfeit illness was called malingering, and the patient so labeled was considered a legitimate object of the physician's hostility. After all, it is our "natural" reaction to feel anger toward someone who tries to fool and trick us.*
>
> **Thomas S, Szasz, M.D.**
> *The Myth of Mental Illness*

One of my neighbors complained about how busy she was visiting her sick mother at a nursing home. The mother had pneumonia. When my neighbor would say she needed to leave, her mother would appear to have more difficulty breathing and complain about it. The mother's exaggeration of her condition would always delay the daughter's departure. Once the daughter left the nursing home the mother would begin breathing normally again.

The eventual consequence of the mother regularly ramping up *counterfeit illness* was that the daughter gradually reduced her frequency of visits. Even though she was really sick, the mother used a form of *counterfeit illness* by exaggerating her symptoms to get her way. The daughter would feel terrible after each visit and equally bad for not visiting her. Using *counterfeit illness* can work in the short run, but this weapon can easily backfire as victims tend to avoid contact with people who manipulate them.

Can't Help Bring In The Groceries

Mark gets very engrossed in watching the Sports Channel and dislikes getting interrupted in the middle of the show. Anytime he is watching a sporting event and his wife needs help bringing in the groceries, Mark instantly greets her with, "Sorry I can't help you honey, my back is acting up again." Once he finally gets off the couch, he always seems able to overcome his pain and suddenly is able to play with his kids.

Inadvertent Speeding

It doesn't matter if the alleged infirmity is real or not for it to be used as a weapon. Jasper had been driving with his 'pedal to the metal' on the interstate. He passed a patrol car while going twenty miles over the speed limit. Jasper expected to be pulled over and was not surprised when he saw the flashing lights in his rear view mirror. He explained to the officer that the only reason he was temporarily speeding was that he had an equipment malfunction with his prosthetic leg.

He told the policeman, "I'm having all kinds of trouble with this new leg the Veterans Hospital made for me. My artificial foot got wedged between the brake and gas pedal. I pulled it out as fast as I could to get the gas pedal to go back up." The officer appeared to feel sorry for Jasper and ended up giving him a warning. Jasper's lying about what caused his speeding was an exaggeration of his real condition, thus a form of *counterfeit illness.*

It wasn't really me who did it, it was some unknown force or some illness that controlled my actions.

Cornelis B. Bakker, M.D.
Marianne Bakker-Rabdau
No Trespassing!: Explorations in Human Territoriality

Phobiarama

Uncle Fred owned the Family Time Cinema until it was demolished to make way for a new freeway interchange. His nephew, Marty, had been working at the cinema since the age of eleven, starting as the cleanup boy. For seventeen years Marty learned every aspect of movie theatre business. Marty had been managing his uncle's cinema for over eight years when the state took over the property. Three years later, Marty's wife Jasmine worked full-time while Marty was unemployed except for the occasional odd job at Uncle Fred's house. Whenever Jasmine urged him to look for work, he got anxious about interviewing, and never got around to sending in any applications.

One day Uncle Fred called Marty and left a message to let him know that there was a job opening for a projectionist at the new Cinerama. At the end of her work shift, Jasmine returned home to find Uncle Fred's message on their answering machine. She was excited and happy about this job opportunity and prayed that Marty would get hired there. Jasmine hurried down to the pool hall. She told Marty the exciting news and he said, "I'll take care of it first thing in the morning. I've got to concentrate on this game. Go home and get dinner ready and we can talk about it then." Marty wanted his friends to know that he ruled the roost at home. Later that night Marty got an earful from his wife as she didn't like the way she was treated at the pool hall and wanted to make sure that he did not let this job slip away.

In the morning Marty was panicking about going to his very first job interview. He called his uncle and asked him if he would go to the interview with him. Uncle Fred told Marty that he needed to call the Cinerama and schedule the job interview. Marty told his uncle that he was feeling too anxious to make the call and asked his uncle if he would make it for him. His uncle sighed and said, "I'll make it right away but only you can do the interview." Fred continued, "I've typed up a good letter of recommendation and with your experience you have nothing to worry about. Just put on your old theater uniform and look confident."

Minutes later, Marty found out that the interview was scheduled for three o'clock that same afternoon. Instantly he felt nervous about being interviewed. The more negative scenarios he conjured up in his mind, the more nervous he became. Finally after working himself up into a state of high anxiety, he started to sweat and his chest began to tighten up. He got his neighbor to rush him to the hospital. At four o'clock that same day the ER doctor said he was just experiencing anxiety. The doctor gave him some Ativan and sent him home.

In this story, Marty was able to use the Social Weapon *counterfeit Illness* to get his uncle to schedule his interview. Years of exaggerating his nervousness as a way to avoid getting a full-time job could have been a factor in the manifestation of his anxiety attack. Jasmine said, "Marty, the only thing you get nervous about is having to work". In reality, there is a fuzzy distinction between real and counterfeit illness. Sometimes only an experienced clinician can tell if the person is demonstrating a pattern of behavior that leads to a desired result, or a "real" anxiety disorder which could benefit from professional help.

Chapter 7

PSYCHOANALYSIS

The term *"psychoanalysis"* was developed by Austrian physician Sigmund Freud. It proposes that the unconscious mind strongly influences everyday behavior. *Psychoanalysis* became the predominant method for comprehending behavior and dealing with mental instability during the first half of the twentieth century.

Psychoanalysis becomes a Social Weapon when people try to convince us that they understand our mental reasoning better than we do. Once we decide to let ourselves become analyzed by others, we are more likely to become trapped by their explanation of our behavior. *Psychoanalysis* is used to cause us to doubt our reasons for taking a position or acting a certain way. This Social Weapon works by getting us to answer questions that usually begin with "Why". These questions are designed to get us to question our own reasoning. The self proclaimed expert then tries to undermine our answers with a more valid sounding explanation.

The Textpert

Jay had a friend named Molly who loved to spend hours on her computer and cell phone. She primarily used her cell phone for text messaging and would have multiple conversations going on at once. Jay enjoyed talking on the phone and would often call Molly.

During one of their conversations, Molly asked him, "Why don't you learn to text?" Jay replied, "I like talking to you on the phone because it's more personal." Molly answered, "If you give it a chance and learn to get better at it, you'll find that texting can be just as personal as talking!" Jay let out a big sigh and said, "I can't picture texting as ever being the same as talking, and isn't it a health hazard spending too much time in front of a screen?"

Molly paused and gathered her thoughts and confidently said, "I think that any side effects were linked only to the old screens. You might not be aware that texting has been shown to prevent Alzheimer's disease by keeping the mind from getting too lazy. Are you someone who only looks at the negative side of things? Someone as smart as you should be able to easily see that the health benefits obviously outweigh any possible downside. What is going on in your mind that makes you so text phobic?"

Jay thought for a while and finally acknowledged, "Well I guess I have issues with the impersonal nature of modern technology." Molly raised her voice and said, "I see what your problem is, but it doesn't work for me. In this day and age, I really don't have time to constantly have phone conversations with my friends. I need to stay in touch with everyone I care about without wearing myself out talking on the phone all day. Why is it so difficult for a well-meaning technophobe like you to see my point of view? I want you to explore your fear of texting, and when you are feeling stronger, text me with your findings. I've got to go now, good-bye!" CLICK.

This story illustrates how *psychoanalysis* is used to help the questioner get his way. It was not really about who was right or wrong. Molly's use of questions loaded with the weapon *psychoanalysis* combined with *ridicule* begged for responses that would set Jay up to fall into the trap of being out reasoned. She would use his answers or lack of answers to logically analyze him from her own point of view.

> *Logic is neither a science nor an art,*
> *but a dodge.*
>
> **Benjamin Jowett**
> **English Educator and Greek Scholar**

Sex Therapy

Part of my work at the University of Washington Department of Psychiatry included a stint as a sex therapist. The sex clinic was quite busy as mainstream medications like Viagra had not yet been invented. Dr. Bakker, the program director, assigned me to work with a couple named Hugh and Margaret. The couple was hoping to solve Hugh's erectile dysfunction. Hugh attributed his lack of performance to fear of his wife's put-downs. This psychological form of impotence could often be resolved when both parties cooperated together when following the clinic's established protocols.

During the sessions, Margaret would often bring up topics that Hugh did not want to discuss. When this happened, his Social Weapon of choice was to confront criticism by asking psychoanalytic questions. He would reactively say something like, "Why do you constantly have to put me down?" Hugh was literally asking Margaret to examine her own mind to figure out why she wanted to upset him. He might not have really wanted his wife to explain her reasoning to him. His attempt at using the Social Weapon *psychoanalysis* did little to help Hugh show that his impotence was being caused by Margaret's use of *ridicule*.

Margaret was unfazed by Hugh's question, so he decided to use another form of *psychoanalysis* to try to get the advantage. Rather than ask Margaret for a reason, he told her what her reason was by saying, "I know why you wanted me to come here. You're still mad because I gave your mother a piece of my mind." Margaret coolly responded, "This has nothing to do with my mother, this is about your impotence." Hugh now lowered his head and said, "See, I knew you were out to embarrass me." Then as if on cue Margaret would lay into him with *psychoanalysis*: "Why do you have to get so defensive about everything? I know why! You want to avoid the real issue, your drinking, and how it leads to your problems in bed." First, Margaret hit Hugh with a question analyzing his defensiveness and then followed with a seemingly rational explanation of why he is impotent. Margaret was able to out manipulate Hugh by being more expert at the weapon *psychoanalysis*.

The habitual use of Social Weapons has become an accepted way of coping with modern problems. Remaining peaceful is difficult when other people continue to attack us. Hugh and Margaret developed the habit of negating each other's statements with *psychoanalysis*. Both of them operated under the assumption that they were preemptively defending attacks. This psychological Social Weapon use gives us attention and advantages, yet these dubious rewards come with a price. If we create bad feelings to get what we want, undesirable consequences often await us. The habit of subjecting others to *psychoanalysis* often increases our chances of being disliked and retaliated upon. This couple would have been better off listening to each other instead of blaming each other.

The Movies

Marsha had just crawled into bed early for a good night's sleep. Her husband Josh walked into the bedroom and asked Marsha, "Would you like to go to the movies tonight?" Marsha closed her eyes and pleaded, "Please, not tonight." Josh asked, "Why not?" Marsha placed her head on the pillow, yawned, and said, "It's miserable out and I'm too worn out!" Josh, acting oblivious to Marsha's need for rest, announced, "This is a great opportunity to wear that new winter coat that cost us $450.00. You'll be warm as toast." Marsha coughed and said, "It's not just the cold. I don't feel that great." Josh softly said, "OK honey, why don't you take a nap? I'll do the dishes and later I will check to see if you're up to going to the eleven o'clock show." Marsha turned her head away from Josh and mumbled, "Let me get a full night's sleep and maybe we can see the movie tomorrow." In the middle of her muffled statement Josh slammed the bedroom door and hurried to the kitchen.

After about ten minutes an angry Josh returned to the bedroom and turned the bright overhead light on. Marsha was in dreamland when Josh shouted, "I know the real reason why you don't want to go! It is about that important sales presentation I had to make at work. Wasn't that the night that you wanted to see this movie? You're still mad about that aren't you? This is your way of getting even with me, isn't it?" Marsha, reacting to being so rudely awakened, asked, "Why are you being so paranoid? Why do you think I'm trying to get even with you? Which voice in your head thinks that I want to upset you? How many ways must I tell you that tonight doesn't work for me?" Josh pointed his finger at her and said, "Why don't you admit that this is your way of getting back at me for the other night?" Marsha pulled the covers over her head and muttered, "Right now I just need sleep." Josh replied, "What makes you think the movie will still be showing by the time you want to see it?" Marsha shouted, "Listen if this movie is so damn important to you, why don't you take the new winter coat on a date to the show?"

Josh had disregarded his wife's exhaustion as he mindlessly used the Social Weapon *psychoanalysis* on her in a botched attempt to get his way. She countered with *psychoanalysis* and *ridicule.* These two weapons are often paired together for an even more derisive effect.

Psychoanalysis works because most of us are socially conditioned to answer questions. We don't have to explain why we think what we think, do what we do, and feel what we feel. Sometimes there are no questions asked. *Psychoanalysis* is about claiming to know a person's fundamental motivations in order to take charge of them.

Chapter 8

FOR YOUR OWN GOOD

For your own good is based on framing the positive in order to hide the negative. It is not unusual for people to try to manipulate us by convincing us that they are better at judging what is good for us. Even when we recognize the Social Weapon *for your own good* being used against us, it can be awkward to reject an offer of help. *For your own good* often comes in the form of advice. For example, a neighbor could say, "You might consider pulling the weeds in your yard now during the spring when the ground is still loose."

<u>Getting To Know You</u>

After I served as a social worker at a neurosurgery center in California hospital I was promoted to the position of organizational development specialist. At the end of my second week on my new job my boss, Luna, called me into her office. She explained, "You are going to be dealing with many personalities and problems. I think it would be good for you to meet as many people at the medical center as you can. The sooner we can make this happen the better. I have a great idea how to help you do that." She put me in charge of organizing the United Way Campaign.

Luna had been running the United Way Campaign for six years straight and decided to pawn off the added work to me. She was able to frame this burdensome task as an opportunity. In order to benefit herself she indicated that running the campaign was for my own good.

Black Belt Shenanigans

Timmy was seven years old and had been diligently practicing the martial art Aikido for three and a half years. During class Timmy generally acted under control and his instructor Sensei Kentaro considered him a good example for the other kids. Timmy was invited to observe the Black Belt tests and promised his grandfather that he was going to really pay attention to the process. Those being tested had spent an enormous amount of time and sacrifice preparing for what was an important event in their lives. The testing was being video recorded and any distracting activity around the mats would be considered very disrespectful.

It turned out that the two kids sitting next to Timmy were intent on playing and goofing off. Instead of keeping his promise to stay focused on the testing, Timmy was lured into joining the other kids' fun. They were doing all they could to make each other laugh as they made faces, pulled their shirts over their heads, and succeeded in getting attention from those participating in the testing. Timmy's grandfather noticed some of the frowns directed at the kids, and quickly approached Timmy about his behavior.

Timmy's grandfather told him that this was a good opportunity to stand out in a favorable light to Sensei Kentaro. He whispered, "With these other kids acting out of control, this is your opportunity as the highest ranked kid to set a good example and earn the respect of the other members of the dojo. Later you will see that acting accordingly will help you advance sooner to the next rank. You know Sensei Kentaro always considers behavior as an important factor for deciding to test."

Timmy listened to his grandfather because advancing in rank was the most important thing in his life.

For your own good is a way for manipulators (and parents) to direct a person's perspective. It works best when emphasizing the benefits. This minimizes the disagreeable aspects of a particular action or task.

Chapter 9

SMOKE SCREEN

The Social Weapon *smoke screen* takes us off our issue by obscuring the definition of the situation, or tangentially bringing up irrelevant information, or responding off topic.

Persons in positions of influence often use their station to *smoke screen*. Common red flags for this Social Weapon are 'I know better than you' and 'Given that I'm an expert at this' and 'Just trust me.' One of the ways that *smoke screens* work is by steering us away from our areas of expertise. Once we are focused on an irrelevant issue or distorted information, it becomes difficult for us to state our case without appearing foolish.

The Chimes of Death

This is a story about how Molly successfully navigated past a *smokescreen* that appeared to be a dead end. When Molly moved to Portland, Oregon, her old Macintosh computer quit working. This was very upsetting for her as she was short of money and was desperate to do some e-mailing. To get the computer fixed she took it to a large computer store. At the store a salesman named Harold asked if he could help her. After Molly explained her problem, Harold said. "Let me see if I can get our technical advisor to help you." After several minutes, Marvin, the tech expert, appeared and picked up the computer. Marvin invited Molly and Harold to follow him into the Tech Room. Marvin plugged in the computer, hit some keys and a chime began to go off. Marvin and Harold looked at each other nodded their heads and said in unison, "The chimes of death!" Harold immediately went back into full tilt sales mode and consolingly said, "I'm sorry to give you the bad news. It looks like you are going to have to buy a new computer. The good news is that you came on a day when we are having a sale!"

Molly was very attached to her computer and did not buy into the chimes of death *smoke screen*. She asked Marvin and Harold, "Where can I find someone with the expertise needed to bring it back to life?" Harold looked apprehensive as Molly kept following Marvin the tech expert around the store. She was relentless in badgering him for an answer to her question. It took less than fifteen minutes for Molly to pry the answer she was looking for out of Marvin. She thanked him for his help and quickly navigated past Harold who was now pitching a couple who appeared to be serious buyers.

A half hour later Molly dropped her computer off at a small place called the Mac Shop. The owner said, "It should be ready in a couple of days." The next day, Molly received a phone call with the news that her 'dead computer' was back with the living! The cost was $39. The problem was just a loose wire. By ignoring the salesman's *smoke screen* and persistently asking for what she wanted, Molly was able to accomplish her goal. The type of *smoke screen* used on Molly typically misleads its victims by exaggeration and misrepresentation.

Messy Guests

One of my students, Joan, called me to laugh about a simple *smoke screen* used on her by a friend. She had just spent considerable time, effort and money remodeling the guest area in her house. Soon after the remodel, her first visitor, Ruth, arrived to spend the weekend. On the first day, after lunch, Ruth took off for sightseeing. Joan went into the guest area to see if anything needed straightening up. She found Ruth had left sopping wet towels and a bathmat on the bathroom floor, and left all the lights on.

She complained to Ruth and was expecting an apology. She was surprised to hear her friend respond by saying, "What kind of flooring did you put in? A bathroom floor should be able to hold up to moisture." Ruth's simple *smoke screen* redirected the issue from what behavior should be expected of guests to what kind of floor a responsible homeowner installs. Joan just said "It doesn't matter what the floor is made of. Guests should pick up their wet towels and turn off the lights."

Chapter 10

SEDUCTION

The Social Weapon *seduction* entices or beguiles its victim as a means of acquiring control. Companies that fought against government regulation at the turn of the twentieth century would say, "Leave us alone and we will create prosperity for you." The type of *smoke screen* they used was 'trust us' and the type of *seduction* they used was the promise of prosperity. It is not unusual for these two Social Weapons to be used in combination.

Piled High

Benjamin was really hungry. He had been running errands on an empty stomach all day. When Benjamin finally arrived home, his wife suggested they walk a few blocks to a pancake house, "It will be fast and easy," she said. So they walked in the restaurant and were seated. On the table Benjamin noticed a plastic sign. It showed a photo of a French dip that looked big and juicy. In bold letters the description said, 'piled high'. He did not even look at the menu. A French dip piled high was just what he wanted. He could almost taste it.

Fifteen minutes after Benjamin placed his order the waitress arrived with the food. He looked at his French dip sandwich and his heart sunk. It was a small bun containing one paper thin slice of meat. He spoke right up. "It's supposed to be piled high!" and he pointed to the picture on the sign. "Oh, that's how our cook always makes them," said the waitress as she rushed off to another table. Benjamin was warned by his wife not to throw a fit. Twenty years later when he told us this story Benjamin was still upset about his *seduction* by the misleading picture of the French dip sandwich.

The big print giveth and the small print taketh away.

Tom Waits
American Musician

Big Shot

Jerry Smith had been working as a handyman at Big John's Athletic Club for over ten years. His wife held a prestigious position at a prominent university. Jerry often felt intellectually inadequate when encountering members of his wife's social circle.

At work, Jerry encountered status-conscious clientele who were reluctant to converse with the hired help. He once remarked to his wife, "Those snobs at the gym make me feel like I'm just another piece of exercise equipment!"

One day Jerry was reading the paper and noticed a job opportunity that promised rapid advancement for the right applicant. The job title was listed as being a regional executive engineer for a large chain of athletic clubs. Jerry decided to apply for the job and was hired. His responsibilities included overseeing maintenance of the fitness equipment at seventeen different locations in a five state area.

Under great pressure to perform, Jerry struggled to keep up with his new duties. His paychecks were larger than before, but he had to pay nonreimbursable living expenses while constantly being on the road. He ended up contributing less than he had in the past to his family's shared income.

Jerry was overwhelmed by the never-ending repairs and was uncomfortable making quick fixes on equipment. The pressure to have everything up and running fast caused him to compromise the quality of his work.

While driving between locations, Jerry often found himself daydreaming of being at his old job where he could take his time and ensure that things were done right. During the hiring process, Jerry had been promised a support staff. Months later, when he brought up the subject of getting assistants, he was seduced again when told, "It's coming soon. Just hang in there."

Jerry had been misled by seductive promises of assistants and future advancements. He had acted like a big shot when he resigned from Big John's Athletic Club and felt he could not go back.

Chapter 11

SEX

The Social Weapon *sex* is the giving or
withholding of sexual favors to control conduct.

*Sex often becomes a vehicle for the attempt at
domination; one partner often uses it to
dominate, manipulate, or tear down the other.*

Myron Brenton
Sex Talk

Affairs Not of the Heart

Tammy attended one of my Peaceful Self
Defense System workshops. While the Social Weapon
sex was being explained, a light went on in Tammy's
head. She began to share how her husband Pete was
using that Social Weapon. I was shocked when she
said, "Well, anytime I go against Pete's wishes he goes
out and has an affair. He then comes home and tells me
all about it. He gets real mad and blames me for having
forced him to find other women. He says that all the
money he had to spend could have been saved if I had
just done what he wanted." Tammy was being
manipulated to believe that she had no choice but to
comply with all of Pete's requests.

Too Much

Cindy and Jack were newlyweds. During their honeymoon Cindy asked Jack about his sexual history. She wanted details of his previous relationships and explained that if he was honest with her it would only make their marriage stronger. After hearing about his prolific sexual exploits, Cindy insisted that they make love daily. She often wanted to make love two or three times a day. At first Jack thought he had hit the jackpot. However, the thrill began to wear off. If he refused her in bed she would become angry and ask him if he had been with someone else.

This situation caused them to fight to the extent that they sought out a marriage counselor. Cindy explained her insecurities to the counselor, "If I make love with Jack all the time he won't have the energy for someone else." Cindy did not trust her husband's marital fidelity. Driven by a lack of trust, Cindy decided to constantly use the Social Weapon *sex* to keep Jack from cheating on her.

Wham Bam Thank You Sam

According to Sam, his first wife Marilyn was seldom in the mood for making love. She seemingly lacked romantic feelings. She had no interest in his seductive communication. Nor did she ever want to engage in cuddling, kissing, or foreplay. However, when Marilyn was in the mood for sexual intercourse, she would expect an instantaneous and solid performance from Sam. Marilyn would habitually act displeased no matter how well Sam performed during their infrequent sexual unions. If Marilyn needed something from Sam outside the bedroom she would tell him that he would later be rewarded in bed. Her controlling manner in the bedroom is an example of the Social Weapon *sex* being used to get her way. This form of manipulation caused Sam to experience performance anxiety and to eventually become impotent.

Marilyn's use of *sex* as a Social Weapon was devastating to Sam, as he did not know how to defend against it. Fortunately for Sam, he found a more romantically compatible partner in his second wife, Ann. At the beginning of Sam and Ann's relationship he was still having erectile dysfunction problems. Ann talked him into attending the University of Washington sex clinic. Sam's virility was completely restored after only six weeks of sexual reprogramming. This process was completed faster than normal due to this couple's use of caring communication. Love helped heal the destructive effects of Marilyn's manipulative use of the Social Weapon *sex*.

*Sex as a weapon can and does
lead to impotence and frigidity.*

Myron Brenton
Sex Talk

Chapter 12

COMPETENCE

The Social Weapon *competence* is used to manipulate others to do one's bidding by telling them they are more expert, capable, able, or skilled at performing a certain task. *Competence* can also be used in a reverse fashion to point out a victim's shortcomings in order to keep him from performing a task.

On the Prowl

During his late thirties, Mark appeared strikingly handsome to most women. He worked as an assistant manager at an accounting company. When Mark would step into the local community fitness center, he would transform from a quiet accountant into a pickup artist on the prowl. His preferred to date college-aged women. He was very knowledgeable about the exercise equipment that was available at the community center. He claimed his specialty was teaching women to develop lean athletic bodies. This specialty only came into effect when he encountered women to whom he was attracted. When these ladies showed up at the center, Mark would instantly become energized and do all he could to become their tour guide.

One day a young lady named Mickey from the state college joined the fitness center. Mark immediately set out to convince Mickey that he was just what she needed to achieve her fitness goals. At first Mickey tried to keep her distance from Mark, but he was relentless. He started noticing the small mistakes she was making in her training and began to show her how she could improve her workout. Mickey became less confident in her abilities to properly train herself and decided to let Mark hang around her for the rest of that training session. At this point Mark had successfully used the Social Weapon *competence* to enter her world.

A Big Flop

Julie knew that if she did not step up and direct her daughter's high school graduation dance it could end up being a big flop. Having been involved with several projects with the other parents she could visualize them making a mess of things without her.

Julie realized that organizing the dance would entail a lot of time and work. At first, Julie was reluctant to get involved in this thankless undertaking. She had very little private time in her life as an overworked parent. However, Julie felt that she was the only parent competent enough to properly run this event and decided she had no choice but to volunteer.

The graduation dance was a big success. But, Julie's private time was severely compromised. Julie used the Social Weapon *competence* on herself. She talked herself into taking on this burden in order to ensure that her daughter had a good time at this important event.

Chapter 13

DRESS

The Social Weapon *dress* is used as a form of appearance or disguise to gain preferential treatment. We dress to create an image that gives us the upper hand. In addition, our body language and choice of words can enhance (or undermine) our appearance. This Social Weapon can be employed by merely looking down our nose at someone or by using the right kind of facial gesture that helps us influence others.

Along with dressing up their physical appearance, effective politicians have long been able to manipulate, dominate and control others by using the appearance created by their words. This form of the Social Weapon *dress* can be used to mount attacks as well as hide unpopular agendas. Thomas Jefferson, the third U.S. president, was known as someone who seldom found himself without the right words. His rhetorical skills regularly helped him overcome verbal onslaughts as he carefully dressed his speeches to gain favor from his listeners.

In matters of style, swim with the current;
in matters of principle, stand like a rock.

Thomas Jefferson

It Was As If I Didn't Exist

Dr. W. Edwards Deming was a giant in the field of management theory, statistics, and quality control. Dr. Deming spent decades trying to help business leaders understand how management is responsible for creating fear in the workplace. He showed how fear can undermine productivity, paralyze innovation, and destroy trust among workers. He maintained that American management had walked off the job. In the 1950's, Dr. Deming created a business model that was introduced to the major Japanese automakers after being ignored by most American businesses.

Early one Sunday morning, Bob, a management consultant, and a lawyer friend named Bruce had an appointment to interview Dr. Deming. Bob picked up Bruce so they could ride together to meet Dr. Deming. Bob knocked on Bruce's door and was invited in. Bruce was casually dressed. Bob was dressed in his best business suit. Bob asked Bruce, "Don't you think it would be a good idea to wear a suit and tie?" Bruce replied, "It's Sunday morning, being casual should be okay. No one dresses up on weekends anymore." Bob pleaded, "I'm lucky to get this interview and I would really appreciate it if you could put on something a little more professional." Bruce said, "O.K." and pulled a sweater on over his polo shirt. Bob was still not happy but figured there was no getting through to Bruce.

Dr. Deming seldom granted interviews. Bob had good reason to worry that Dr. Deming at ninety years of age might take offense that he brought someone along with unsuitable attire for the occasion. The two friends arrived on time and were invited in by Dr. Deming's secretary. Bob and Bruce spent over three hours interviewing a very stoic master statistician. Bob reported that Dr. Deming never spoke to or even looked at Bruce. Even if Bruce asked Dr. Deming a direct question, Dr. Deming's answer would be directed to Bob. Driving home after the meeting Bruce said, "It was as if I didn't exist."

A few days later Bob was doing some follow up work with Dr. Deming. As he was getting ready to leave for home, Bob got into a conversation with Dr. Deming's secretary. Bob came to find out that the secretary had worked in the home office for thirty-two years. During all those years, she had never once seen Dr. Deming dressed without a coat and tie.

When we are dressed improperly for an occasion we run the risk of not being taken seriously. Bruce's choice to appear informal created an unintended show of disrespect. Dr. Deming reacted to the perceived slight with a cold shoulder routine. When at important meetings or other social occasions, we can always 'dress' down later but we can never 'dress' up.

Party Crashers

Dressing up can help people wield power over others as in the case of Tareq and Michaele Salahi, who crashed an event at the White House. The Salahis exposed how the Social Weapon *dress* overcame one of our country's best security teams. They were uninvited guests who were dressed to the hilt. Their presentation included beautiful attire and confident smiles. The Social Weapon *dress* helped them masquerade as dignitaries and stroll by the Secret Service to attend President Obama's first state dinner. If the Salahis had been dressed like our lawyer friend Bruce there is little doubt they would have been stopped at the door.

Smiles are also a form of *dress*. When we wear friendly smiles like the Salahis, other people sense that we are not a threat. According to Richard Conniff, in his book *The Ape In The Corner Office*, smiling comes from thirty million years of primates practicing their fear grin, or signaling that they are not a threat.

The Grateful Beggar

There was a destitute looking man in dirty tattered clothing who sat in front of an upscale grocery store near Beverly Hills. Every day from 3:00 pm to

7:30 pm this impoverished looking soul would sit on a stuffed gunny sack with a sad look on his face. When anyone gave him money, he would always reward them with a thankful smile and say, "God bless you!" Looking so woefully miserable helped him get paid. Making a production out of his gratitude allowed his donors to feel good about themselves. One of the people who would regularly donate to him was a grocery clerk named Brad.

One day Brad was having an after work drink with his girl friend at a popular bar close to the grocery store. From the vantage point of his table he noticed the same beggar slip past him with his gunny sack to the men's room. Fifteen minutes later the beggar, now freshly groomed and well dressed, sauntered out of the restroom and headed out the back door. He had transformed his filthy image into a clean well-groomed one. Brad later told us, "I couldn't believe what I saw. He was wearing such good looking threads." Brad hurried to the back door in time to watch this successful panhandler hop into a flashy sports car and drive off. When Brad returned he asked the bartender about the guy. The bartender confided that the beggar's name was Herb. He went on to tell Brad that every Friday he would get a twenty dollar tip for letting Herb change there that week.

Herb's choice of *dress* for the location turned out to be an effective weapon for manipulating others to pay him. When Herb rewarded his donors with a grateful looking smile he was using a form of the Social Weapon *dress*. Herb's sincere appearance of gratitude would help obligate his ever-growing clientele to make him their regular charity.

Protecting Women

In some male dominated societies, women are required to wear a burqa and purdah when outside their homes. A burqa is a loose fitting outer garment that covers the entire body. The purdah is a veil that conceals the face. The purpose of this attire is to stay out of the view of men who are not immediate family members. This particular outfit has been described by cultural critics as a weapon used by men to dominate women. Some of those who disapprove of this mandatory clothing describe it as a yoke that curtails a woman's freedom to have a public identity. Many of the wearers of these traditional garments defend their use. They see this attire as a form of protection. By using the Social Weapon *dress* they are able to maintain their anonymity while in public.

> *Oh prophet, please tell your wives and daughters and faithful women to wear a covering dress on their bodies. That would be good. Then nobody can recognize them and harass them.*
>
> **Sura Al Hijaab**
> *The Qur'an*

91

Chapter 14

GIFTS

Gifts is the Social Weapon of indebtedness. It is used to make victims feel obligated to the manipulator. When someone's charitable offering is accepted, it becomes easier for the giver to pressure the victim for something in return. Sometimes people use *gifts* so they can feel entitled to deliver abuse.

Having The Book Thrown At You

Early in this book there is a story titled 'Mao's Giant Hand.' It is about how Dr. Long helped me get a perspective on how I had created a big drama out of the unexpected actions of a guy named Ned at the gym. I became subject to the Social Weapon *gifts* as soon as I agreed to accept a book he thought I should read.

My friend Bill and I were having a discussion about how many people our age were having trouble keeping up with all the new technological advancements. During our talk Ned interrupted us. He said he had two copies of a book on that very same topic and wanted me to have one. A few minutes later I happened to mention to my friend April that Ned was giving me this book. April said, "You'll be really sorry if you let Ned give you his book." I did not heed April's warning. The next day Ned gave me the book.

A few days later I crossed paths with Ned who was in a foul mood. He informed me that he was mistaken and had only one copy of the book and wanted it back. I asked, "When will you be here next? - I'll be happy to return your book." Ned gave me a frown and then said, "I'll be here Wednesday, you know I'm always here at 10 a.m. on Wednesdays!"

On Wednesday at the appointed time, I arrived with Ned's book in hand. Ned was nowhere to be found. After an hour of waiting, I explained my situation to Heidi, the physical therapy assistant who worked at the gym. Heidi said she would put the book in a safe place and keep an eye out for Ned so I wouldn't have to waste my time waiting for him.

A week later I encountered Ned at the gym. I smiled and asked Ned, "Did you get your book back?" Ned's face turned beet red as he looked at me and began to belittle me with statements laced with obscenities about how I failed to return his book.

The people observing this scene were stunned. The manager of the gym opened the physical therapy office and got Ned his book. Ned took the book and continued with his Yosemite Sam routine, jumping up and down while 'swearing a blue streak.' I later learned from other members that Ned had a drinking problem and that his behavior often fluctuated from nice to nasty. I then thought, "Sure wish I had listened to April and not taken the book."

The power that Ned obtained by giving me the book was nullified after he took it back. Following Ned's outburst, I did not feel any indebtedness to be social with Ned. If Ned had refrained from the way he took the book back, I would have felt an obligation to continue to interact with him. Later that day, I observed my own mind using Social Weapons against myself as I mentally revisited the event and continued to make myself feel miserable. I knew I was making matters worse, but my thoughts were dominated by the vehemence of Ned's actions. Later, Dr. Long helped me realize that I was making a mountain out of a molehill. In hindsight, I am glad the meltdown took place. Since Ned's blow up, I have been cautious about accepting *gifts* from acquaintances.

Free Massage

Margie and Donald were colleagues working the graveyard shift at a woolen mill. During one of their breaks, Margie complained to Donald about the difficulty she was having getting her required amount of hours practicing massage. She needed three more hours to complete a massage class that was required for her to get licensed. Donald asked, "You mean you can't find people to practice massage on?" "That's right," replied Margie. Donald said he would be happy to let Margie practice on him. She set up the first of three massage appointments with Donald.

Later that week Donald got his first massage. He believed he was doing Margie a favor and at the same time was hoping the massage would be pleasing. Donald later confided, "She seemed to have a good sense of touch, but she wouldn't stop talking about all her problems. I was sure glad when it was over and didn't have to listen to her anymore."

A couple of weeks after receiving his third massage, Donald received a call from Margie. She told Donald a good way he could pay her back for the massages was to let her use his swimming pool. Margie arrived the next day to use the pool with her three children in tow. Soon her family was regularly hanging out in Donald's backyard, swimming in the pool, running into the house, using the bathroom, and invading Donald's privacy.

Donald operated with limited Social Weapon awareness, and unclear boundaries that increased his vulnerability to Margie's manipulative attack. Had he been more aware, he would have known to ask up front, "Are there any strings attached to my getting this massage?"

Donald could have set boundaries at the beginning by asking Margie, "I want to make sure this practice massage is considered a favor to you. Let me make sure I'm understanding this correctly. Are you asking to practice massage on me without my owing you anything in return?" That way Donald would not have to worry about any recompense as he could always remind Margie of the deal she had made with him.

The insidious Social Weapon *gifts* can be hard to recognize. Only *gifts* that obligate us to the giver need be considered Social Weapons. Many charitable people give weapon-free gifts while expecting nothing in return.

Charity or philanthropy can work just like the Social Weapon *gifts* when resources are given to a family down on their luck, a business that needs resuscitating, or a third world country that has financially collapsed. The hidden agenda of the givers is sometimes one of gaining more control over the receivers. Independence and autonomy are at stake when *gifts* are used as Social Weapons.

The Social Weapon *gifts* can also be used in a reverse fashion, which is called charity. Instead of giving something we are asking for something we feel entitled to.

Picture the new neighbor coming over and borrowing something from our kitchen. We are glad to comply and wish him a pleasant evening. As times goes by, we are asked for more and more favors. Charity becomes unending as the needy neighbor continues to ask for more food, gardening tools, trash bags, and car errands. His demands will continue if 'a line is not drawn in the sand.'

Chapter 15

OVER THE BARREL

Over the barrel is a Social Weapon that attempts to put its victims in a hopeless position. It is the act of being pressured under duress to comply with another party's threat or command.

Over the barrel can come in the form of blackmail. It is commonly used to coerce us into doing something we do not want to do by giving us undesirable options. It can place us in fearful predicaments and powerless situations where others are in control. This Social Weapon reduces our choices to the extent that we feel forced to submit to the manipulator's wishes or take uncomfortable risks. Even though *over the barrel* is a very effective Social Weapon, those who use it are taking the chance of destroying relationships, starting interpersonal wars, and initiating feuds.

German Revenge

Successful use of the Social Weapon *over the barrel* often leads to retaliatory behavior. Nations or people who see themselves as victims of this Social Weapon can be consumed with hostility. The historian Margaret MacMillan, in her prizewinning book *Peacemakers: The Paris Peace Conference of 1919 and Its Attempt to End War,* tells how the Germans were told they had no options but to accept the World War I peace treaty. MacMillan further explains that the seeds that led to World War II were sown at that peace conference.

Once the Allies had the Axis *over the barrel*, they took advantage of the situation by exacting a retaliatory sentence on the Germans. Germany was given no choice but to accept harsh terms that threatened their country's pride while decimating their economy. The treaty lacked any conciliatory clauses and was mired in vindictiveness. This use of the Social Weapon *over the barrel* would prove to be a factor leading directly to the Second World War. Hitler reminded his countrymen how the allied countries had stepped on them. He fanned the winds of war by weaving the theme of revenge and patriotism in his rousing speeches to uncover and unleash the German citizens' underlying hostility. If the Allies had not exacted such a high price for Germany's participation in World War I, Hitler could have had a harder time manipulating his countrymen. The consequence of this manipulation was over seventy million people dead, many more injured, a huge cost in resources, major environmental damage and untold suffering.

<u>Schmoozing Off the Barrel</u>

In George J. Thompson's book *Verbal Judo*, he describes how he avoided being put *over the barrel* during a hostage situation. A man was demanding a million dollars and an airplane in exchange for his hostage. Thompson, who was the police negotiator at the scene, responded by saying, "So do I!" (want a million dollars and an airplane) and Thompson laughed. He began his negotiation with humor to help calm a volatile situation. Thompson succeeded in keeping communication alive and was able to forge a bond with the perpetrator and convince him to give up his hostage. Thompson managed to keep from using Social Weapons to get his way and avoided triggering a violent reaction. Apparently, his friendly approach kept his humor from being taken as *ridicule*.

Dr. Bakker's Diagnosis

Dr. Cornelis Bakker was the psychiatrist in charge of the Adult Development Program at the University of Washington. The program delivered mental health services using an educational rather than medical model. When a person came into the program wanting to change an aspect of his behavior he would receive the label 'student' rather than 'patient'. Dr. Bakker believed that being diagnosed as a patient with mental problems could lock a person into a role where change would be difficult to achieve. As students, people were free to experiment with trying out different unfamiliar behaviors. When making incidental mistakes during this process the 'students' were able to escape the detrimental effects of psychiatric diagnosis.

Dr. Bakker believed that giving people a diagnosis was counterproductive when it came to changing behavior. He felt patients would act out according to whatever diagnosis they had received. After the word got out, the Department of Psychiatry demanded that all students coming through the program must be given a diagnosis. Dr. Bakker could easily have become a victim of the Social Weapon *over the barrel* if he had bought into this ultimatum. Dr. Bakker, however, held a staff meeting and explained the problem and its solution. The staff was to give all students the same diagnosis: "Adult Situational Reaction." He complied with what the department of psychiatry wanted. At the same time he got what he wanted - no labels.

Gunpoint at One a.m.

When I was a skinny young teenager, I worked the night shift at a gas station in the south central part of Los Angeles. My boss was undefeated during his time on his high school wrestling team. This record does not count the many times he was disqualified for excessive violence. He said he enjoyed hurting his opponents more than winning. Recently, he had hospitalized the Army's heavyweight boxing champion in a street fight. It was not unusual for my boss to come back to work and wash the blood from his fists to his elbows, and the blood was seldom his own. He was mean to everyone and I was scared to death of him.

One night four large men confronted me with a handgun and demanded that I open the gas station safe. They instantly put me in a position of being *over the barrel*. If I did not comply with their wishes, I might get killed. I was afraid of them but was more terrified of what my boss would do to me if I gave up any of his money. Even when the boss was not present, he controlled me with fear which is often a component of *over the barrel*.

I knew my boss would be back at any moment and decided to try to slow down the situation. I started out by playing dumb and acted like I didn't understand what they were asking me. The result was that the men became more agitated. The man with the gun told me in a threatening manner that I better open the safe. I had overcome my initial state of shock and mustered up some semblance of courage. I took a deep breath, looked the gunman in the eyes and said, "I can't. The boss has the key!"

Seconds later (which seemed like an eternity to me), the boss entered the side door. Before anyone knew what was happening he started throwing oil cans at the would-be robbers. His aim was accurate and the cans hit the robbers with great force. The men panicked and ran out the door. The boss chased them off the lot while cussing and causing bodily injury with each can thrown. My boss had reversed the roles and placed the gunmen *over the barrel*. And I had learned very quickly that I did not like being held at gunpoint, working for a violent boss, and in both cases, being *over the barrel*.

The Little Shrimp

At the Little Shrimp Restaurant, Bruce had been promoted from dishwasher to busboy. When Bruce was being trained he was shown the mop and bucket and was given details of how to clean up at the end of his shift. Bruce said that as a busboy he shouldn't have to clean the restrooms. The manager told Bruce that if he didn't he could forget working at the Little Shrimp. Bruce was put *over the barrel*, decided to suck it up and work hard at doing his required duties of being a busboy/janitor. Eventually Bruce worked his way up to become a waiter and fifteen years later became the restaurant's manager.

One day I was applying for a summer job at the Little Shrimp. During my interview, the manager Bruce told me that my job would include cleaning the toilets. He further explained his success story began with cleaning the restrooms. Bruce had been put *over the barrel* and rather than lose his job he complied with his manager's wishes. Cleaning toilets didn't faze me and I wasn't experiencing any symptoms of being placed *over the barrel*. I just wanted the job. Bruce ended up hiring someone he liked better. I ended up being hired by a boss with a violent reputation at a gas station where the restroom was kept locked with an out of order sign on the door.

Over the barrel works as a Social Weapon only if the victim feels compromised and forced into an undesired position that allows no easy way out. Having been used to cleaning my family's toilet when growing up, I would have accepted the restaurant job without feeling manipulated by the Social Weapon *over the barrel* like Bruce apparently did.

Chapter 16

GUILT

The Social Weapon **guilt** is used to convince others to feel uneasy or under obligation for their actions. It can create shame, regret, and low self-esteem. We turn the Social Weapon **guilt** on ourselves when we fail to recognize the manipulation. **Guilt** is so socially ingrained that most of us accept this Social Weapon even when we know we are being triggered to beat ourselves up. Its effectiveness relies on our accepting the manipulator's viewpoint.

> *Guilt, so commonly used in our society to manipulate and punish, manifests itself in a variety of expressions, such as remorse, self-recrimination, masochism, and the whole gamut of symptoms of victimhood.*
>
> **David R. Hawkins, M.D., Ph.D.**
> *Power vs. Force*

Christmas Is Family Time

During holidays the Social Weapon **guilt** is often used. June and her husband Sam were a young couple living in Seattle. One year they decided to spend Christmas with their friends and do some skiing close to home. June's parents resided in Southern California while Sam's parents lived in Arizona. In the past, the

Seattle couple had made a tradition of visiting both sets of parents during the Christmas season. This year they had decided to stay home to save travel expenses and see what it was like to enjoy Seattle at Christmas time. They also felt that taking a break from their usual journeys might be good for their relationship. They decided to call their respective parents and let them know about their intentions well ahead of time so their relatives could plan their holiday without them. They made their calls and immediately began to feel pangs of uneasiness as their parents worked them over with *guilt*.

During the phone calls, they began to feel that maybe they didn't have the right to break their family tradition. Listening to their parents, they were reminded that Christmas is a family owned time. **Guilt** was induced by Sam's mom when she said, "I guess if you're not going to be here, we won't bother to have a tree or turkey or any of that stuffing you like." June's father was even more merciless when he said, "It's all right if you don't want to come home, but don't forget that your grandmother isn't getting any younger and, after her surgery this year, she may not live to see another Christmas."

<u>You're So Mean</u>

Jeff and his wife Lana raised their grandson Hugo. When Hugo was six years old he was already a pro at using *guilt* on his grandparents. When he didn't get his way, he usually went into a tirade of how badly he was being treated.

Jeff usually succeeded in changing Hugo's mood by telling him, "You remember how to turn your mad channel back to the happy channel don't you? It is just as easy as turning the channel on the television." If that failed to do the trick, Jeff sometimes tried to change Hugo's perspective by saying, "Your behavior might work on some other people, but it doesn't work on grandpa." Using the Social Weapon *guilt*, Hugo would typically stick to his issue and reply, "Everyone else gets to go out and have fun and you are going to make me stay here with no friends to play with. You're so mean! I hate you and I love Grandma Lana the most."

Self-manipulation with the Social Weapon *guilt* only compounds and perpetuates the effects of the Social Weapons others use against us. When being verbally attacked by Hugo, Jeff caught himself feeling guilty for not being able to satisfy all of Hugo's perceived needs. In order to escape the grip of negative emotions, Jeff sometimes followed a protocol for dealing with Hugo. It included kindly smiling at his grandson while observing the nature of the Social Weapons that were being used. Jeff improved his chances of keeping his composure by becoming an observer.

Occasionally when Jeff was concentrating on an important project, Hugo would interrupt him. One time as Jeff was under pressure to finish a project, Hugo told Jeff he wanted to go to his friend's apartment building to play. Jeff reminded his grandson how he loved him and then he said, "At your age it would be dangerous for you to run loose where bad people might do something terrible to you. The police are always being called to that apartment complex and if I let you go there by yourself, Family Services might take you away from us. You don't want to be the cause of that happening do you?"

Jeff's attempted use of *guilt* was rendered ineffective when Hugo countered with, "I can't wait. I probably would be treated better with someone else in charge anyway." Jeff then decided to take more time to evaluate Hugo's requests. He finally got Hugo to compromise with him by saying, "If you decide to control yourself and stop bugging me for one hour, I will take you and your friend to go do something fun before soccer practice. Right now I have no choice but to get my work done."

Kind and Calm

Awareness of *guilt* induction is useful for avoiding uncomfortable emotions. In order to maintain a sympathetic state of mind, it helps to look at our attackers as people who have fallen into the habit of using Social Weapons to get what they want. Even a small amount of compassion for the Social Weapon bearer can direct our attention away from emotional reactivity. By remaining in an understanding state of mind it is possible to direct our attention to the attacker's behavior and escape from being drawn into his drama. Remaining calm is key to clearly examining our options and effectively responding to behavioral attacks.

Recognizing another's manipulative behavior allows us the mental space needed to consciously respond instead of allowing our emotions to take control of our thoughts. This approach relies on remaining kind and not taking things personally when we catch someone attempting to use *guilt* on us.

> *When you refuse to take things personally, you avoid many upsets in your life. Your feelings of anger, jealousy - and even your sadness - will simply disappear if you don't take things personally.*

> **Don Miguel Ruiz**
> *The Four Agreements*

You Make Me Sin

Melinda had been divorced from her husband, Hank, for over a year. Hank had one day per week visitation rights with their children. Hank would periodically take advantage of spending part of a day with his kids. When he returned them to Melinda's house, he used that brief time to try and convince Melinda to have sex with him. When Hank behaved this way, she would ignore his advances, tell him his five minutes were up, and usher him out of the house.

About an hour after being rejected, Hank would typically telephone Melinda and inform her that he once again was forced to look at pornography to relieve his sexual tension. Hank firmly believed that viewing pornography was a sin. He would go to great lengths to convince Melinda that her rejection of him was making him sin. He would say, "If you would just go to bed with me once in a while, I would not have to keep on sinning." After about 20 seconds of this, Melinda would hang up the phone.

During their marriage Hank manipulated Melinda with *guilt*. Now that they were no longer married, Hank's desperate and unconvincing use of this Social Weapon had little impact. One of the reasons Melinda left Hank was that she had grown weary of his manipulative behavior. For a while, she had used the Social Weapon *guilt* on herself by feeling obligated to stay married even though she viewed the marriage as a big mistake. She used to feel that their continued union was best for her children. Now that she was free of any obligations, Hank's attempts at making her feel guilty only reaffirmed that she made the right choice in divorcing him.

Talking Cattle

In *The Gentle Art of Verbal Self Defense at Work*, Susette Haden Elgin, Ph.D. explained how language barriers have confined us. In the book's chapter, Malpractice of the Mouth, she wrote the following paragraph:

111

"Let me offer a few encouraging words, to be referred to when progress seems slow. Let's talk cattle for a minute. The only reason cattle can be confined by an ordinary barbed wire fence is that they have no idea they can jump over it. If they ever do, by bizarre chance, jump a fence even once, they are liberated cattle thereafter. No ordinary fence will ever hold them again. People are precisely the same way about the language barriers that verbal abusers set up to hold them back. The only reason such barriers work is that people have no idea they can get past them. A person who does get past, even once, is no longer a prisoner of verbal abuse in the same way. And such barriers will never hold that person back in the same way or to the same degree again."

Throughout her marriage, Melinda had faced a continuous barrage of the Social Weapon *guilt*. Melinda felt trapped like one of Haden's confined cows until she recognized the hollowness of being blamed for Hank's shortcomings. Once free from those illusions, she recognized her options, empowered herself, set boundaries, stopped taking Hank's issues personally, and reclaimed her freedom to feel good about herself.

Chapter 17

DEFINITION

The Social Weapon *definition* is the labeling of a person or situation. *Definition* can be difficult to identify because it is often a natural part of talking:

"I've never been able to be on time." People use this to continue being late and to continue stealing our time.

"You seem like a reasonable person." People often say this just before stealing our territory.

Definitions can be endless:

I've never been able to control my temper.
I never get any help around here.
You're impossible to get along with.
Having dinner with your family is boring.
Reading this will make you uptight.
You are too critical of people.
I'm just trying to be helpful.
When I call you names it's out of love.

Definition is regularly interwoven with other Social Weapons. Most of us depend heavily on this Social Weapon for influencing the behavior of other people. Everyone has experienced being pressured into adapting their behavior to conform to a given *definition*.

Definition is one of the most commonly used Social Weapons. It is the labeling of people or situations. This Social Weapon is used to manipulate others by defining things in a way that makes its victims vulnerable to control. Many Social Weapons can be considered forms of *definition*. In the case of the Social Weapon *flattery*, we might define others as being generous. If we can get people to perceive they are generous, we are more likely to get what we want from them. The Social Weapon *ridicule* is a type of *definition* used to belittle others. The Social Weapon *helplessness* often consists of defining one's inabilities in order to avoid performing a task.

> *Definition of the situation is the*
> *overriding determinant of behavior.*
>
> **Charlotte Booth, MSW,**
> **Executive Director**
> **Behavioral Scientist Institute**

We tend to structure our behavior in a way to be in conformity with our given definitional labels. For instance, when my friend Dick played college football his coaches referred to him and his fellow teammates as scholar athletes. This labeling was used by the coaches to remind the team they had responsibilities outside of the playing field. This form of subtle manipulation was used to encourage athletes to keep their grade average up. Higher grades were needed to maintain the football players' athletic eligibility.

How we define ourselves controls how we think, feel, and behave. Most of us have a tendency to define ourselves as we believe other people see us. The opinions of others can bait us to accept a self-limiting (or self-aggrandizing) perspective. Our personal choices are reduced every time we take this bait. This curtailing of our freedoms is usually an insidious process. Our best chance to avoid this manipulation is to be wary of the labels given us.

Definition can be difficult to identify because *definitions* are a natural part of all conversations. We become prey when we are persuaded to believe in someone else's *definition* that undermines our best interests. We limit our choices anytime we accept labels without question.

He Is So Greedy

Definition can control future thoughts. Paul and Jill met while they were ironing out the terms of a financial contract that involved millions of dollars. Jill had hoped that part of the commission being divided would go directly to a charity of her choosing. Paul negotiated the contract in such a way that he eliminated her charity from being in the equation. Paul reasoned

115

that each person receiving a cut of the funds would be free to donate to whatever charities they wanted and should not be forced into giving to any cause not of their choosing. Jill did not know that Paul anonymously allocated his entire share of the proceeds to create a trust fund that helped disadvantaged inner city kids.

Jill was thinking only of her own charity and became angry at Paul for eliminating it from the commission pool. She thought Paul was trying to get a larger commission by cutting her charity. Her view of Paul was based on the belief that he was being selfish. This inaccurate *definition* of Paul trapped Jill into casting all future thoughts of him in an unflattering light.

Paul was secretive with his generosity when it came to helping others. Most of his colleagues loved him and admired his big-heartedness. For almost a decade Jill continued to gossip at her office about Paul's greed. Co-workers who knew Paul would be astonished by her assertions and come to his defense. They would tell Jill numerous stories of Paul's unselfish acts. Jill would turn a deaf ear to any evidence that depicted Paul as a generous person.

Most of us have made a habit of gullibly accepting the first *definition* that fits our current view of reality. This expedient process simplifies our lives as it gives us the illusion that we can predict other people's future behavior.

It can take a very convincing knock on the head to change one's habitual point of view. Even if Jill had been shown irrefutable evidence that Paul had donated his entire share, she still would have had a difficult time redefining him as a generous person. Labels are easy to give and hard to shed. We tend to fight against redefining what we have already established as truth. Only evidence that supports our *definition* is viewed as acceptable.

A Cooked Wife

Julia prided herself on being a great cook. This opinion was strongly influenced by her husband Adam who constantly reinforced that image with his compliments. Adam owned an insurance company and was budget conscious. Every year he persuaded Julia to cater his company's Christmas party. One year the company made huge profits and Julia saw it as a chance to take a break from cooking. Julia asked Adam if he would consider using a professional caterer, or take the employees out for the holiday meal. He responded by saying, "Honey, it would never be the same. Everyone looks forward to your delicious home cooked Christmas dinners. We can't disappoint our employees." Julia bought into her label as being irreplaceable in regards to the company's Christmas party. She felt she had no choice but to put in long hours in the kitchen to keep the employees from being let down.

Adam not only defined Julia as being a superb cook, he also defined the situation in such a way that she bought into the trap of being indispensable to the success of his Christmas party. She felt compelled to do the duties that are inherent in being a great cook and a good wife. Julia's belief in her label as being indispensable to the success of the holiday party limited her freedom to take a break from cooking. This was the seventh year in a row that Adam used the Social Weapon *definition* to cut costs on his holiday party. As with all Social Weapons, people usually use the manipulation that has worked on their victims in the past.

Free To Be Myself

Ernie, a family therapist, was working with a married couple named Rob and Dottie. In the counseling session Rob would fly off the handle and berate Dottie at the drop of a hat. Dottie would then turn away from Rob and clam up. She would say nothing more unless Ernie asked her a direct question. After one of these verbal beatings, Ernie asked Rob, "Why do you talk to Dottie like that? Can't you see how upsetting it is for her?" Rob replied, "I have to express my anger, or I would never be free to be myself." Rob was operating under the assumption that needing freedom gave him the right to verbally abuse his wife. Ernie asked Dottie if she wanted to comment on Rob's behavior. "No," she replied, "If I ever say anything he always gets so mad." Rob used *definition* to give himself the freedom to abuse his wife. Dottie defined the situation in a way that kept her a victim.

Mass Manipulation

Definition has been used to control entire populations and delude decent people into harming others. Leaders throughout the centuries have used the Social Weapon *definition* to involve countries in wars and their inherent atrocities. At the Nuremberg war trials of 1945-46, the head of the Nazi Party, Hermann Goering, explained how those in power manipulated an entire nation. Goering said, "The people can always be brought to the bidding of the leaders. This is easy. All you have to do is tell them they are being attacked and denounce the pacifists for lack of patriotism exposing the country to danger. It works the same in every country."

The Social Weapon *definition* has forced populations to accept perspectives that in normal circumstances would have been deemed unacceptable. Those who voice opinions that might undermine the intentions of a ruling power are routinely branded as being unpatriotic.

If we base our rationalizations for killing on a label, we run the risk of compromising our responsibilities to one another. In order to create a blind allegiance with willing warriors, governments intentionally begin programming their citizenry at a young age with patriotic catch phrases and slogans. Those who see through these insidious *definitions* are harder to manipulate.

Recognizing Social Weapons can help us learn to see the varied and unconscious ways we fall prey to labels. People depend heavily on using the Social Weapon *definition* for influencing behavior in their life situations. When we accept these labels it makes us easier to manipulate.

> *Our perceptions are essentially distorted by our own self-definition, which in turn is qualified by identifying with our limitations.*
>
> **David R. Hawkins, MD., Ph.D.**
> *Power vs. Force*

Chris the Crooner

The Social Weapon ***definition*** can take away our freedom. This happened to me when I was happily singing at school with my classmates. My fourth grade teacher undermined my confidence to sing by defining my singing abilities.

The class was rehearsing for a big musical presentation. Mrs. Holland had a sickened look on her face as she raised her hand signaling the class to stop singing. When the room was quiet she pointed right at me and said, "You sound terrible Chris. You have no talent for music whatsoever. Do not sing with the rest of the class!" She went on to tell me to only mouth the words in order to avoid ruining the entire production.

Shocked into believing that I was a lost cause when it came to singing, I refrained from trying anything musical for a long time. As years passed, I continued to define myself as musically inept and avoided exploring my musical capabilities.

The Social Weapon *definition* (combined with
ridicule) robbed me of future musical participation by
forcing me to relinquish my personal power. During my
most formative years I was forced into believing a self-
defeating label. This distorted view lasted for more than
fifty years before I regained the power to take up a
musical instrument. With a friend's encouragement to
learn to play the hand drums, I decided to give it a try
and enjoyed it. This helped me shed the self-limiting
label that was imposed during my childhood.

The Social Weapon *definition* works against us
when it negatively narrows our perception and reduces
our choices. A common ploy used to control us is the
assertion that we are either a certain way or its opposite.
Our controllers might say that we are either with them or

against them. They might tell us we really don't care about them if we do not continually profess our love. They might claim that we must be lazy and self-centered when we decline to do what they ask.

Definition can manipulate the thinking of a nation, a company, a family or an individual. Defining words influence the way everyone thinks and behaves. Once defined, we can be mentally shackled to conformity.

When we catch others using *definition*, we recognize that we have a choice to reject another's point of view.

No fight Social Weapons

The final three Social Weapons in this section fall under the banner of passive-aggressive behavior. These Social Weapons are indirect expressions of hostility. They can be described as passive resistance to complying with someone else's expectations. These Social Weapons give the user the ability to fight by appearing not to be fighting.

Chapter 18

PRETENSE

Pretense is the Social Weapon that uses a deception in order to manipulate another. It can come in the form of deceiving another with false promises. The user misleads or lies about what they are going to do. He has no intention of following through and then if confronted says he is getting around to it soon. *Pretense* is often seen after the fact as a delayed lie or empty promise. It can also be likened to the spider's seemingly harmless web that is used to trap its prey.

> *Will you walk into my parlour?*
> *Said a spider to a fly;*
> *Tis the prettiest little*
> *parlour that ever you did spy.*
>
> **Mary Howitt**
> *The Spider and the Fly*

Pretending To Be Interested

At Big John's Gym, Joe had a friend named Carter, who was an extremely dedicated bodybuilder. Joe liked working out with Carter because he always showed up on time and did not miss workouts. One day a charming young lady named Sarah appeared at the gym. She spotted Carter and quickly interrupted Joe and

Carter's workout. Sarah ignored Joe and began to talk to Carter about her commitment to getting in shape. She explained how she loved the gym and working out. She asked Carter for advice with her workouts. She got Carter to give her a tour around the gym and then asked Carter to have lunch with her so they could continue their conversation about fitness training.

The next day Carter did not show up for his workout with Joe. After about a month of being absent from the gym, Carter stopped by to tell Joe that he was getting married. He went on to say, "Sarah doesn't like the kind of women that hang out at this gym so I bought a Bowflex workout system and I train at home now." Joe asked, "So you're working out with Sarah now?" Carter confided, "No, she lost interest in training. You were my best workout partner ever but you know how it is." Sarah was quite skilled in her use of *pretense*. Pretending to be interested in exercising helped her get just the guy she wanted.

Beware Of Me

One day my friend Tim and I came across an acquaintance named Carol. Carol, with feigned interest, asked me, "How are you doing with your book?" I answered, "My wife Emi has really been busy and unable to help me with the editing lately and..." I was about to continue to explain how my friend Doug was helping me with the writing and how well I felt the book was progressing when Carol cut me off. She smirked and said, "Now you're blaming getting nothing done on your wife. Why don't you just give up and admit that you can't get it done!"

As we exited the scene, Tim looked at me and said, "Man, that was really unpleasant! Why did she act like that?" I explained, "Carol was using the Social Weapon *pretense*. She pretended to be interested in how the book was coming along with the sole intention to berate me. Usually I manage to avoid talking to her. Her mode of operation is to suck her victim in with mock friendliness and then lower the boom." Tim started to laugh and said, "What's her problem? She should wear a BEWARE OF ME sign." His humor was contagious and as I laughed I felt Carol's negative energy leave me.

I Promise You Won't Regret It

After Tom's divorce my wife Emi and I let him stay at our house. Tom said that he would only be there long enough to find a place of his own. He ended up staying for months and contributing nothing for the arrangement. He failed to honor his share of the expenses and chores after pretending he would pitch in. He constantly raided the refrigerator and made sure there would be no leftovers after any meal. After six months of being an immovable and unwanted object, Tom found a girl friend and moved out of our place. Tom married the girl friend and the marriage lasted about six years.

Following his second divorce, Tom called me and pleaded, "Could you find it in your heart to let me move in for a short time?" Tom's request brought up the pent-up hostility that I had held on to from his last stay and I said, "Well, that last six months of you vegetating in our house was miserable for everybody." Tom used *pretense* again saying, "Just tell me what chores you want me to do and I'll do them!"

I really wanted to believe him. I explained the situation to Emi who just rolled her eyes and said, "It will be exactly like it was before." Tom fooled me, but not my wife. She had Tom's number and saw right through his use of the Social Weapon *pretense*. As Emi expected, after Tom got his foot in the door, he instantly reverted to his lazy freeloading ways. When a friend asked how I could fall for the same lies again, I told him, "I genuinely believed that Tom had changed his ways and I can't believe I let myself be used like that again."

Chapter 19

PACIFISM

Most of us have heard about or experienced people who parasitically avoid getting a job, neglect paying their portion of rent, or escape doing a fair share of chores. People who have wormed their way into this type of arrangement often use the Social Weapon *pacifism* to maintain the status quo:

> "Whatever you say is okay with me."
> "I'll do whatever you want."
> "It's not worth fighting about."

The person using this social weapon appears to be peaceful, but in reality they are being passive-aggressive. There is no follow-through on promises. "Whatever you say" is not really okay and "I'll do whatever you want" means nothing. The Social Weapon *pacifism* works best on people who fear confrontations.

The pacifist often remains so calm that the victim of the weapon easily becomes irritated and hostile. It is difficult to defend against a pacifist because we always feel we are having to attack.

The Social Weapon *pacifism*, in addition to maintaining the status quo, can also be used as a strategy to bring about change. This powerful Social Weapon was successfully used to draw attention to social injustices by reformers like Martin Luther King and Mahatma Gandhi. Through the use of *pacifism*, they improved conditions for the downtrodden and oppressed.

> *Since being in India, I am more convinced than ever before that the method of nonviolent resistance is the most potent weapon available to oppressed people in their struggle for justice and human dignity.*
>
> **Martin Luther King Jr.**
> **1959 Radio Address**

The Green Bean

Herman had grown tired of being a tavern owner and was desperately trying to sell the Green Bean Public House. After several months of having his business on the market, Herman finally found someone willing to buy the Green Bean. The timing was bad that week as Herman's landlord Peter notified Herman that he had just sold the building that contained the Green Bean. To make matters worse the new landlord, Mr. Tate, was going to raise the monthly rent. Herman became upset and began to worry that this rent increase might undermine the sale of his business.

129

One of the Green Bean patrons suggested that all Herman had to do was to get Mr. Tate to delay raising the rent until after the business was sold. Herman was not a skilled negotiator and had always relied on his physical prowess to get his way. On the way to Mr. Tate's office, Herman got himself worked up to the degree that his head was bright red and the look in his eyes was one of hatred. Herman purposely walked through some garden soil before storming through Mr. Tate's waiting room. The Persian rugs wore his boots' imprints as he began shouting at the office personnel and shoved a chair out of his way before cornering old man Tate in his plush office.

Herman loudly said, "You need to come up with a better lease. If you mess with me, I'm going to mess with you. If the Bean sale goes bad because you raised the rent, you are going to regret ever trying to screw me over!" The implied threats were obvious. Mr. Tate remained unfazed, smiled and said, "You are someone I would never want to mess with. I'm an old man and I have trouble getting around. All I want is to get along with my tenants. One of the reasons I bought the property was that you have an excellent record of paying the rent on time." Herman lowered his voice a notch and interjected, "Yeah, I pay on time and for that I get screwed over."

Mr. Tate paused and then lowered his voice even more saying, "Didn't Peter tell you that he was going to increase the rent when the lease is up next month? Peter told me that he had everything worked out with you and that you thought this minimal increase was no big deal." Mr. Tate then continued in a compassionate tone, "Oh, I think I see what happened. I will call Peter and look into this situation for you. He described you as a reasonable fellow and never shared with me that you were getting ready to sell your business. I'm sure the people buying the Green Been are already aware that the lease is about to expire and this small increase should make no difference to them."

Mr. Tate went on, "I was really looking forward to keeping you as a tenant. From all I have heard about you, once someone gets to know you, that you are really a good guy. Now, I'm expecting my great granddaughter here any minute. I wish I could spend more time with you." Herman sheepishly replied, "I have a few more errands to take care of anyway. You know, the bar business has really taken away my positive attitude."

Mr. Tate was able to soften Herman's demeanor by using *pacifism* and avoiding arguments. His soft voice and geniality seemed to suck all the anger out of Herman. He left without negotiating any new changes in the lease while thinking what a pleasant man Mr. Tate was. He didn't realize that the subject of Mr. Tate renegotiating the lease was sidestepped. Herman even picked up a few chunks of dirt off the carpet on his way out as he feared how inappropriate his earlier behavior might have been viewed.

Chapter 20

WITHDRAWAL

The Social Weapon *withdrawal* is aggressive while appearing passive. It is the fleeing from unwanted discussion: hiding from a nosy neighbor, staying under the radar at work, or avoiding an ex-spouse. The weapon *withdrawal* is a sneaky way of avoiding something that presents a problem. If the other party wants us to stick around they learn not to bring up topics that trigger our immediate retreat.

In addition to avoiding an undesirable situation, *withdrawal* can be the act of dealing with others by becoming unresponsive or silent. The following story illustrates how silence can be a form of *withdrawal*.

The Silent Eight

Working as a management consultant for a travel agency, I was asked to solve a personnel problem. The owner, Sylvia, said all of her eight employees had been giving her the silent treatment for about three weeks. Every time she would confront an employee with a direct question, she would get a brief response followed by silence. Sylvia told me, "I'm about to go nuts! I'm running a business here, this has to stop."

To find a solution for Sylvia's problem I arranged a meeting with her employees. I asked, "What's going on with you and your boss?" I found out that Sylvia wanted a paper free office and that the office workers had been told that everything had to be done on their computers. The computer system was new and the employees did not trust it. They had been keeping hand written notes about things they felt were important. The weekend after Sylvia's paper free decree, she had gone through everyone's desk and gotten rid of all her employees' notes.

During the meeting, the employees expressed how they felt violated. All the workers assured me that they were not hostile. Later Sylvia and her staff attended my Peaceful Self Defense System workshop. During the workshop, I made it clear how the Social Weapon *withdrawal* had been used reactively. They acknowledged when their personal notes were destroyed they felt powerless and instinctively used the Social Weapon *withdrawal*. After Sylvia consulted with me during lunch, she stood before the class and apologized for her misuse of power.

Withdrawal was no longer seen as neutral behavior. The workers agreed that they were hostile after I explained *withdrawal* in the context of it being a retaliatory behavior. Some of the staff actually commented that if they had not used such a powerful weapon, their grievances would never have been settled.

Three months later I entered the travel agency to give a refresher class and witnessed a dramatic change in the way everyone interrelated. Sylvia and the staff were having fun together and appeared to be once again on the same team.

Pema Got Stuck

Pema Chodron is a Tibetan Buddhist nun who has written many books that offer fundamental spiritual wisdom. In her compact disc, *Getting Unstuck: Breaking Your Patterns & Encountering Reality,* she discusses how she was emotionally triggered by another person's *withdrawal*. It was a situation in a retreat where Pema felt that a friend was exhibiting hatred towards her by giving her the silent treatment. Pema related how she let the other woman's silence take over her thoughts. Even for Pema who is a master of controlling her ego, it was easy to become hooked by the Social Weapon *withdrawal* in the form of silence.

Silence is the unbearable repartee.

Gilbert Keith Chesterton
English Critic and Author

SOCIAL WEAPONS WRAP-UP

We can catch the onset of social attacks by being aware of the Social Weapons being used. Regular practice of recognizing the 20 Social Weapons is a necessary step in mastering the Peaceful Self Defense System. Understanding the mechanics of how these Social Weapons work provides us with a foundation for peacefully dealing with them. Comprehending how they function allows us to see how our territorial boundaries are being crossed.

> *Weapons are the tools of fear; a decent man will avoid them except in the direst necessity and, if compelled, will use them only with the utmost restraint. Peace is his highest value...*
>
> **Lao-tzu**
> *Tao Te Ching*
> **Stephen Mitchell translation**

Part two, Making Sense of Conflict, will introduce the concept of human territoriality, which is key to understanding human behavior.

PART TWO

MAKING SENSE OF CONFLICT

Chapter 21

THE TERRITORIAL BEHAVIOR PERSPECTIVE

The force called territory as it affects a world
of living beings bears at least one resemblance
to a force called electricity as it affects a world
of apparatus: The substance of each is as
elusive as the effects are spectacular.

Robert Ardrey
The Territorial Imperative

In Part One of this book we described how to identify Social Weapons. This knowledge is necessary, but not sufficient for understanding the sources of most human conflict. The perspective of territorial behavior provides a theory that helps us better understand human desires, needs, tendencies, and boundaries. It explains why all of us behave in such befuddling and conflicting ways.

Having a clear view of why others behave the way they do helps us to protect what is dear to us. In order to widen our viewing lens, we need to know more about the psychology of the human need for territory. My introduction to human territoriality and Social

Weapons occurred when I was a graduate student studying mental health therapy.

Dr. Bakker's World of Human Improvement

After finishing my first year of graduate school in social work at the University of Washington, I had a persistent feeling that my studies were going in the wrong direction. I felt that my training was archaic and ineffective. I decided to talk to my friend Vic about my concerns. Vic had just completed his second year of study in the same graduate program. He listened to me and then suggested I go to the Coach House where they were experimenting with a patient-friendly approach that seemed to be working. I hurried across campus to the Coach House.

The Coach House was the home of the Adult Development Program (ADP). Dr. Cornelis Bakker, M.D. was the founder and director of the program. The ADP was an experimental alternative to traditional mental health treatment. It created a school for patients to learn to become their own change agents. They enrolled in classes rather than groups. It provided those seeking a healthier mental outlook the means to change themselves without being branded or limited by a diagnosis. Dr. Bakker felt that diagnostic labels acted as roadblocks to self-empowering changes. During orientation, students were told that they were going to be studying the most exciting subject imaginable. They were going to be studying their own behavior.

137

New enrollees in the Adult Development Program were taught that behavior was learned and not a manifestation of disease. They were told to see themselves as students of behavior change, not patients. They were shown how counterproductive behavior could be unlearned, and taught to adopt new behavior in its place.

Students were taught to take responsibility for undesirable behavior by creating goals for change. Most students discovered that playing a passive patient role had been counterproductive to their self-empowerment. At the ADP, student experimentation with self-transformation was reinforced, and setbacks and failures were seen as learning opportunities.

ADP students were asked to develop credulous attitudes. This mental outlook was described as a childlike naiveté that was both open and enthusiastic. Once convinced that change was possible, students began to expand their range of behaviors.

Consistent use of a conduct diary was seen as a way to focus on behaviors that needed changing. Students kept track of undesired actions and thoughts. They were taught that writing about what they wanted to change in their lives was an essential step towards personal transformation. By focusing on the content of their writing, students discovered themselves making conscious behavioral adaptations. With writing, the students were able to step outside their usual mind's eye and were able to look at themselves from a more detached point of view. Students reported that while writing in their diary, they regularly experienced thoughtful revelations for self improvement.

I was excited about Dr. Bakker's groundbreaking approach for helping people empower themselves through a series of behavioral changes. My enthusiasm for my chosen field of study was renewed as I immersed myself in Dr. Bakker's world of human improvement.

Chapter 22

THE CONCEPT OF TERRITORIALITY

When I began participating in the ADP program I attended Dr. Bakker's class on territoriality. Dr. Bakker explained how territory crosses all species: It is what we own, or think we own. Suggested reading included Robert Ardrey's *Territorial Imperative, African Genesis,* and *The Social Contract.*

From this class I learned that territoriality is our inclination to own everything from personal property to beliefs, behaviors, and ideas. A key to understanding territoriality lies in the observation of territorial behavior: People claim and mark desired areas, give trespassers warning displays, defend against intrusions, and search for desirable new territories.

> *Territory is that area of an individual's life which he experiences as his own, in which he exerts control, takes initiative, has expertise, or accepts responsibility.*
>
> **Cornelis Bakker, M.D.**
> **Marianne Bakker-Rabdau**
> *No Trespassing!: Explorations in Human Territoriality*

Setting Boundaries

Personal boundaries are territorial limits we formulate between ourselves and others. In order to set clear boundaries, we need to determine what portions of our territory we claim as ours, and what we are not willing to give up. Once we know what it is we are protecting, it becomes easier for us to establish clearly marked boundaries and discourage trespassers.

Whenever our territory is open to intrusion, we need to mark our boundaries by sending warning signals. If we are saving someone a seat at the movie theater, and someone else starts to make a move towards it, we might send out a warning signal like, "This seat is already taken." To keep conflict to a minimum, it is customary to mark the seat (territorial claim) by draping a coat or other belongings on it as soon as possible. Clearly marking property is the primary means of minimizing disputes.

Even without the use of physical markers, the habitual use of a given territory is traditionally regarded as a claim for its continued use. As a teacher of human behavior, I have seen that most audiences of my lectures return to the same chairs during the following sessions. This acquisition of territory (the chairs) happens regularly and is established in a short time span.

To be effective, the marking of our boundaries must be obvious enough to be recognized by those who might want to take what we want to keep. The following is an example of re-establishing boundaries that were gradually breached.

House Rules

Mary worked full time and spent precious little time with her daughter Amanda. She wanted her undivided attention during the dinner hour. When Amanda first got her cell phone she assured her mom she would use it moderately, unlike some of her friends. After a while, Amanda's initial intentions were forgotten as her electronic addiction grew. Amanda got to a point that she was constantly in contact with her friends via email, Facebook, Instagram, texting, and sometimes even talking on her smart phone.

Mary decided to set new boundaries by updating the house rules. The update stated that Amanda must stay off the phone during dinner time. The consequences of not following the house rules would be that Mary would no longer pay Amanda's cell phone bill. She told Amanda to tell her friends not to text or call during dinner. Mary distinguished what part of her territory was being intruded upon and rationally decided on a course of action to maintain her dinner time boundaries.

Mary was not willing to give up her mother-daughter time. She recognized that the Social Weapons *gradual takeover* and *rapid takeover* via the cell phone were undermining their relationship. Mary chose to establish a defined territory and protect it from her daughter who could not imagine life without her cell phone.

Mary reported that seeing the situation in territorial terms made it clear to her. She saw her boundaries being intruded upon. Mary said being aware of her annoyance increased her Social Weapon awareness and she quickly saw the ***gradual intrusion***.

> ***Give him an inch and he'll take an ell***
> (Around 1900 the word ell was replaced with mile.)
>
> **John Heywood**
> **English Writer of Plays and Proverbs**

Dirty Laundry

After thirty-eight years, Martin was elated that his lazy son Jimmy finally moved away from home. Soon after the move, Jimmy visited his parents and surprised Martin by asking if he could do a few chores around the house. About twenty minutes into the chores, Jimmy asked Martin, "Hey Dad, do you mind if I do some laundry?" Martin replied, "Sure Jimmy, go ahead!"

A month later Martin mentioned to his wife, "The food around here seems to be disappearing awfully fast!" His wife then informed Martin that their son had been coming over regularly to do laundry, and usually had a snack while there. She said, "Jimmy said that you gave him your ok."

Sometimes when we make a small concession we put ourselves in a position to give more than we intended. Martin could have minimized Jimmy's intrusions if he had set clear boundaries by saying something like, "Sure, go ahead and use our washer and dryer this time. I really appreciate that you asked me first and didn't take their use for granted."

Territorial intrusions happen when we think it is safe to stop guarding our boundaries. By trying to be the good guy and doing nothing to lay down the rules (boundary markers), Martin ended up hostile towards his son. Like Martin, many of us hope we don't need to define territorial boundaries. We want to avoid conflict and bad feelings. Even though it makes little sense, we tend to feel guilty for letting it be known that we are unwilling to be manipulated.

Social Weapons like *guilt, definition,* and *gradual takeover* often keep us from clearly setting boundaries. Friends and relatives rely on our desire to maintain peaceful relationships with them. Most of us are not willing to pay the price or to prepare ourselves in advance to do the work needed to protect our boundaries.

After learning about the peaceful self defense system, Martin was able to prepare for his next encounter with Jimmy and his loads of laundry. Martin remained calm and confident as he saw Jimmy coming.

The encounter went something like this:

Jimmy: "Oh, hi dad. Mind if I do my laundry?"

Martin: "No son, go ahead and do it this time and thanks for asking first. You know we are struggling to pay our gas bill and I really appreciate you asking me instead of just planning on making a regular habit of doing it here."

Jimmy: "Well, mom said it was ok. What if I just do one load? Would that make you happier?"

Martin: "Go ahead and do all you have since you went to the trouble of bringing it today. Mom thought I had given you permission to continue doing your laundry here but that wasn't exactly what I said. We really can't afford for you to make a habit of doing it here all the time. We love you and want to help. Just make sure you ask in advance, and that you don't do more than one load at a time."

Jimmy: "Ok, thanks."

In this example, Martin succeeded in stopping Jimmy from playing the game of working his parents against each other. Martin established clear territorial boundaries in the kindest manner he could.

Chapter 23

PERSONAL AND PUBLIC TERRITORY

There are two areas of personal territory. They consist of our personal property and our privacy retreat. There are three areas of public territory. They consist of our personal space, the attention we get from other people, and the social roles we play.

Personal Property

Personal property consists of ownership of our thoughts and tangible possessions. These thoughts include concepts, self-esteem, self-image, memories, hopes, dreams, values, prejudices, beliefs, and moods. Tangible possessions include all we own, including real estate, pets, vehicles, furniture, toys, clothing, and appliances. Some of us take this ownership a step further with a perceived ownership of our family and friends.

"No Trespassing" or "No Solicitors" signs are used in an attempt to ward strangers away from some of our territory. We mark our belongings, books, and papers with our names. To help keep our homes clean some of us establish control over our territory by posting a sign at the entry that says, PLEASE REMOVE YOUR SHOES BEFORE ENTERING.

A Good Fence

Earlier in this book, we described how a fellow named Werner had a neighbor whose garden grew larger each year and steadily encroached into Werner's backyard. Werner eventually had his property surveyed and installed a fence after the neighbor's autumn vegetables had been harvested. After the fence posts had established the property line and before the rails were put up, Werner offered to help wheel the garden's top soil to his neighbor's backyard. The fence (territorial boundary marker) instantly solved Werner's battle against the Social Weapon *gradual takeover*. The tact and consideration he afforded his neighbor helped both of them develop increased respect and friendliness towards each other.

> *Good fences make good neighbors*
>
> **Robert Frost**
> *Mending Wall*

Privacy Retreat

At work, our privacy retreats are places we go when we don't want to be disturbed. It could be a restroom, a break room, a stairwell, our car, or an office. These are places where we can escape the company of others. Privacy retreats outside the workplace can come in the form of bedrooms, tree houses, workshops, country trails, and any other place where we can be alone. Some of us create privacy retreats by turning off our phones and electronic devices. Timing is an important consideration to take into account. To avoid problematic people, knowing when to retreat is paramount. Sometimes our retreat can be inappropriate, uncaring, and irresponsible. Hiding in our den when our spouse needs help with the kids is an example of inappropriate timing.

In some mental health facilities patients are subjected to a forced community lifestyle. In response to this subjugation, residents have been known to create their personal privacy retreats by spending hours in bathrooms, under their bed covers, and in other obscured areas to avoid constant staff oversight and interaction with other patients.

Lock Your Door

In Oakland, California I taught a Peaceful Self Defense System workshop for the U.S. Postal Service. I was explaining how our reputation defends us. At that point in my talk, I was interrupted by Ruth, who said "Then I must have a reputation of being too hospitable. My neighbors are always coming into my apartment without knocking." Before I could say a word another class member asked, "Why don't you just lock the door?" Instead of considering that option, Ruth replied, "Where I grew up we did not have to lock our doors!

People should know to knock first." By using the Social Weapon *definition* on herself, Ruth avoided considering a perfect solution for protecting her privacy retreat boundaries. She used a self-limiting form of *definition* when she said, "Where I grew up we did not have to lock our doors!"

Ruth's stubbornness to avoid doing what was required to maintain a privacy retreat boundary illustrates the powerful control of the Social Weapon *definition*. Ruth continued to be controlled by a *definition* that kept her from locking her door to defend her boundaries. Ruth's belief that people should always knock first prevented her from seeing an obvious solution.

Having a place to withdraw from people helps us regenerate. Some people are energized by other people, but some are easily exhausted. For those of us raising children, a privacy retreat affords us opportunities to take breaks and renew ourselves. Former prisoners of concentration camps complained of the agony they had to endure of not having any place to go to avoid the eyes of others.

Many couples avoid arguments by feigning sleep. When subjected to an unwanted social situation, people have been known to close their eyes and meditate. When we find it difficult to meditate we can still shut out the world around us by simply escaping into our own personal thoughts. Just closing our eyes is a way to create a boundary to keep others from directly disturbing our mental privacy retreat.

When out in public many people wear earphones with the purpose of avoiding contact with others. Many times the earphones are kept in place to clearly mark the privacy retreat even when the wearer is not listening to music.

There are diverse methods people use and places they go for privacy. A simple change in our environment can make profound differences in our mental and emotional outlook. As an ultra distance runner, I love to spend long hours training in the deep wilderness. This remoteness gives me a chance to be completely alone with nature. Unpopulated parts of the planet are my preferred privacy retreats for relieving pressure.

Chris Storey's Privacy Retreat

Personal Space

Our personal space is the invisible barrier we create immediately surrounding us. The amount of physical closeness we allow others depends upon who we want in our personal space. Those we trust are granted the liberty to venture further into our private space. Uninvited encroachers of our normal personal boundaries are considered to be trespassers. All animals have clear boundaries for a safe distance to keep from other animals, depending on the threat of the other species. This behavior helps to maintain their survival. The personal space needed by humans varies with culture. When conducting international business, companies provide seminars to prepare their employees to adjust their personal space to different cultural norms.

> *The distance an animal demands between himself and an enemy is of a special sort called "flight distance."*
>
> **Robert Ardrey**
> *The Social Contract*

Personal space varies in size among different cultures and social strata. In parts of Latin America the proximity one shares with others might be less than what is the norm for personal space in some Northern European societies. Many of us who are accustomed to being in close proximity to others generally consider those who keep their distance as being unfriendly or standoffish. Those of us who feel irritated when uninvited people get too close usually define those intruders as being overly pushy.

Conrad Cool

When working for Dr. Bakker I taught a class in which the students experimented with play-acting different life roles. The students quickly learned that when their behavior changed the reaction of the people around them also changed. The object of the class was to dispel the myth that people cannot change. I wanted my students to learn that behavior change could be both easy and fun when approached with optimism.

One of the members of the class, Conrad, had been a violent career felon. He was accustomed to maintaining a large personal space and was wary of intruders venturing into that space. I gave Conrad a role-playing assignment. I wanted him to play the role of someone who was calm, composed, and extremely cool. To assist in his achieving a high state of coolness, all in the class were asked to call him Conrad Cool.

Conrad Cool's assignment was to remain collected and unaffected while making his personal space available to others for an entire month. In addition to opening his own space, he was told to make a habit of physically getting closer to others.

Everything Conrad Cool did was cool. He began to dress cool, he wore cool shades, and began to practice flirting in a cool way with the opposite sex. The only part of Conrad's role that was not cool was his constant invasion of everyone's personal space.

All of the class members had weekly one-on-one appointments with me to discuss their personal progress. Conrad Cool's meetings radically changed with his new role. I became unnerved as Conrad Cool closed in on my personal space. I would end up nose to nose with Conrad Cool as he backed me across the office until I was pinned against the wall. Conrad Cool remained composed. When the month's assignment was over I laughed and confessed to the class that I wished I had given him a different role (or *definition*).

Personal space varies according to the degree of crowding. Being in a crowd tends to shrink our personal space. People who are unusual, frightening, or in authority are generally given more room.

A Sea of People

Harry Harrison's futuristic novel, *Make Room! Make Room!*, was the basis of the screenplay for the movie Soylent Green. He describes what happens when two well-armed policemen of the future exit their vehicle and move through the overwhelming and oppressive crowds of people inhabiting Manhattan. The crowds "streamed by on all sides, jostling and bumping into each other without being aware of it, a constantly changing but ever identical sea of people. An eddy formed naturally around the two detectives, leaving a small cleared area of wet pavement in the midst of the crowd. Police were never popular....the cleared space moved with them as they crossed Fifth Avenue..."

The Elevator Experiment

Dr. Bakker sent me to Seattle's business district to run a series of elevator experiments. I talked my co-worker, Charlotte, into helping me. We would walk into an office building and wait for an elevator that would have other riders present. Then we would step into the elevator and face the other passengers. Elevator decorum dictates that we are to enter the elevator and then turn and face the elevator doors. Instead, Charlotte and I would continue to face the other elevator riders. This quickly created discomfort for the other riders. People would begin to push up against the sides of the elevator to escape the gaze of the two intruders in an attempt to regain personal space. Charlotte later reported to Dr. Bakker, "We parted the elevator passengers like Moses parted the Red Sea."

This story illustrates how quickly people are impacted when their personal space is trespassed upon.

The Attention We Get From Others

Part of our personal territory is the attention we get from others. If someone interrupts a lecture too many times with questions or comments, that person has stolen the lecturer's attention territory. The lecturer has been put into a position of taking the time and effort to control the disruption and regain territory.

We have all had times when a family member or friend would not let us get a word in edgewise during what we thought was a two-way conversation. What usually occurs is that instead of getting our attention, the other party loses it. Most of us go by the rule, "You are going to have to listen to me if you expect me to listen to you." Most of the time when our comments are ignored we tend to become hostile and give less attention to the nonstop talker.

Parents too often don't listen to their children. Because of this, when a parent tries to communicate with their children, what they say falls on deaf ears. Communication is a two-way street. If we listen to our children, there's a good chance they'll listen to us.

A performers' ability to control a crowd and keep their attention is instrumental to success. Having a public meltdown due to an inability to handle the Social

Weapon *ridicule* and other audience distractions has hampered many a career. The performer who can command control over an audience gains respect from his listeners.

Lou Rawls

The late Lou Rawls was an American jazz and blues singer. He was known for his smooth vocal style. One evening Lou was performing in a Los Angeles nightclub. Several members of the audience were inebriated. They were talking so loud that they were competing with Lou for the audience's attention. Lou stopped the band and spoke calmly into his microphone: "Everyone else came to be entertained by the band and I wish those of you disturbing the audience with your talking would either stop or leave the room." Those who were trying to listen to the music enthusiastically applauded Lou's taking charge of the situation. The skillful and confident manner in which Lou defended his territory resulted in the disrupters remaining subdued for the remainder of the performance.

Roles We Play

Our social roles are conducted based on how we define ourselves in relationships with others. A partial list of these roles include boss/employee, parent/child, police/citizen, male/female, coach/athlete, and doctor/patient.

The roles we play come with action territories. These are areas of activity that we claim as our own. Examples are the space, tools, and skills for cooking or growing vegetables. In these action territories we feel some degree of expertise, responsibility, and control. Some of us prefer status-seeking roles that give us more power while others prefer playing roles that come with less responsibility.

Many roles are not taken on by choice but by necessity. We may not want to do the dishes, clean the house, or discipline the children. Sometimes there are situations that influence us to take on undesirable roles. To maintain our claim on preferred roles, we need to manage **our action territory** well.

Drunk Surgeon

I had a challenge when I worked as an organizational development specialist at a medical center in California. One of the surgeons had become a liability. The other physicians and nurses talked privately about how he had a drinking problem that affected his performance. He had already attended a mandatory substance abuse program to no avail. A group of doctors began to refuse to work with him in the operating room. His drinking caused them to boycott their roles as colleagues rather than working with the offending physician. None of the boycotters wanted to be the one to blow the whistle on the drunken surgeon.

I was given the assignment of finding out why no one wanted to be on the ostracized surgeon's operating team. I met with the other doctors and they revealed the problem they had with the shunned physician. After documenting the interviews, I provided the chief physician with my account of why the doctor was being boycotted by his colleagues. The report included how this doctor had been avoided and protected by his peers. After a few ineffective warnings to the alcoholic surgeon, the chief physician had no choice but to dismiss him.

The code of silence shared by the drinking doctor's inner circle was influential enough to interfere with many members of the medical staff properly managing their work roles. Their fear of taking action further put patients at risk.

The point of this case is that the inebriated surgeon's behavior not only jeopardized his patients, but also affected the work roles of his colleges. The other doctors and nurses let themselves be put in a bind that interfered with their territorial roles as responsible health care professionals and mandatory reporters.

Master Mechanic

Many of us have been annoyed by co-workers who make it hard to get our work done by dominating the use of shared work tools. A mechanic's work can be delayed by missing tools. In order to ensure their ability to perform their work roles most master mechanics have learned to make their territorial boundaries clear by engraving their tools with their names. This labeling of personal belongings to prevent losses that interfere with occupational roles is a common practice at many work places. Experienced mechanics often take this marking of territory one step further when they encounter new workers. They successfully manage their territory by taking the uninitiated aside and in no uncertain terms warn them that they will NOT tolerate anyone, under any circumstances, borrowing their tools.

Lunch Litter

Julia worked as a project manager for a large corporation. Due to limited office space, cubicle sharing was necessary. Almost every day after returning from lunch, Julia would find another worker, John, had been at her work station. He used her computer to video chat with his friends. John liked to eat as he typed and would

160

invariably leave crumbs and wrappers all over the keyboard and desk. Julia began to have an emotional meltdown after months of experiencing growing hostility towards John. Julia angrily told John to stop using her computer. John growled, "It's not your computer. It belongs to the company."

After the confrontation with John, Julia became very upset and decided to start making a plan to defend her territory. She began documenting the problem. Julia took before and after photo shots to provide evidence of each mess John made at her desk.

After two weeks of documenting the disaster zone with her camera, Julia asked for a meeting with John and their boss. When John began to deny what he was being accused of doing, Julia produced a written transcript. It documented the conversations that took place regarding John's insistence he had the right to use the equipment.

As a final closing argument, Julia handed the keyboard photos to her boss and said, "Average clean up time after John is 10 minutes. If John continues to make these messes daily for another year, I figure the company will lose over 40 hours of my work time." The boss gave John a long disapproving stare and said that from now on Julia's work station was off limits to him.

Knowing what part of our territory is being invaded makes it easier for us to succeed in maintaining our boundaries. Julia recognized the weakness of staking her defense on claiming sole control of company property (the computer or her cubicle). Julia won her case by pointing out that her work role (a form of ownership) was being undermined by John's actions.

Shared Ownership of Territory

Shared territory is property that is owned by more than one person. Examples of social unions with shared ownership of territory are business partners, spouses, siblings, communities, tribes, and teams who use, occupy or control common domain. This type of joint ownership gives us less control than sole ownership of any given property.

My Road

As citizens with driving privileges, we share ownership of our highways and roads. When I was driving home from work one day last year, I found myself following a car that was being driven erratically by an elderly man. I thought, "This guy is driving like he owns the road!" Finally, both our cars came to a stop at a red light. I then noticed a bumper sticker on the other car. It read, "YES, I DO OWN THE ROAD!" My perspective was no longer centered on being annoyed as I laughed about the absurdity of the situation.

When we try to take sole ownership of shared property we are likely to attract unwanted consequences. The erratic driver who believed he owned the road put himself in a position to easily become a victim of another's road rage or to a traffic officer's ticket book.

Conflict over shared territory is typically the rule rather than the exception. This conflict is more likely to occur when there is a lack of clear guidelines. People get along better when all parties have agreed to follow a set of rules by which to live and work.

Summary of Human Territories

It pays to memorize the following breakdown of human territory because, once we know the territory involved, it becomes much easier to identify our issue of concern:

1. Your private life

    a. Personal property - everything you own
    b. Privacy retreat - a secure private place
    c. Your thoughts and feelings

2. Your public life

    a. Personal space surrounding you
    b. The attention you get from others -
       psychological space
    c. The roles you play - leading to
       action territories

Chapter 23

TERRITORIAL BEHAVIOR

Territorial behavior includes our thought processes and physical actions when managing, protecting, and acquiring territory. This conduct includes aggressive, protective, and hostile behavior. Mismanagement of our territory results in unwanted stress and emotional reactivity.

Aggression

Aggression is any action we take that attempts to expand our current territory. In the territorial model, even the broadening of our knowledge or the honing of our persuasive skills are considered forms of aggression. They are considered so because they expand territory. More provoking forms of behavioral aggression are the acts of trespassing, stealing, invading privacy, or undermining someone in authority. One recurring example of a role being undermined is when a government or business official is publicly discredited by the press. Another example of this type of aggression is when someone has gone around another to a higher authority to get his way.

Aggression across our boundaries usually relies on the use of Social Weapons. The feeling of agitation when we experience social annoyance is a good indication that our territory is under attack. Anytime we are taken outside our comfort zone, we can use the other's aggression as a reminder to ask ourselves questions that help us reveal the nature of the underlying conflict. What weapons are being used against us? What parts of our boundaries are being crossed? Is it our property, privacy, or personal space? What choices do we have to mitigate the intrusion? After understanding what is occurring we have a better chance of maintaining our territory. In Part Three of this book we will provide the reader with viable options for defending these types of territorial attacks.

You might remember the story about Melody who used whining as an aggressive form of *gradual takeover*. Melody's incessant whining would get her out of many of the roles she was expected to play. When we are unable to put a stop to unrelenting whining, our nervous system can become overwhelmed and exhausted to the extent that we find ourselves surrendering just to stop the whining. If we don't know what to do about this form of aggression, we typically drop our inadequate forms of resistance and let the whiner win.

Aggression grows greater if it does not draw retaliation.

Robert Ardrey
The Territorial Imperative

165

A common mistake most of us have made during territorial attacks is to inadequately defend against or ignore an initial aggressive attack. Failure to act is what allows bullies, cons, and thieves to flourish. Being 'asleep at the wheel' gives the all clear signal to aggressors and the onslaught will escalate. This regularly occurs in situations from geopolitics, to the corner grocery store, to personal relationships. It is wishful thinking to assume that giving up part of our territory will keep trespassers from wanting more.

Hitler's Aggression

A costly historical example of unstopped aggression is Hitler's invasion of Czechoslovakia. In 1938, Great Britain's Prime Minister, Neville Chamberlain, naively believed Hitler's aggression could be appeased by letting Germany take part of Czechoslovakia. Hitler promised that his territorial takeover would end with that one concession. Germany continued to build its war machine and six months later Hitler demanded another large portion of Czechoslovakia be sacrificed.

Chamberlain threatened Hitler by proclaiming that Britain and France would take military action against Germany if he continued his aggression. Chamberlain mistakenly believed his threat of war would stop further invasions. His warnings of retaliatory warfare fell on deaf ears. Hitler's war advisors had little respect for Britain's armed forces and its willingness to wage war against a mightier force. Britain and France had failed to adequately gear up to be a threat to Hitler's well-prepared armed troops and their superior weaponry. The Germans wasted little time crushing Czechoslovakia while suffering few repercussions from the rest of Europe. This lack of consequences led to German troops invading Poland next. Great Britain, and the rest of Europe, experienced the nightmare of World War II because no one stopped the Germans during the early stages of aggression.

On the home front, domestic violence begins to thrive when the first abusive attack is not met with an adequate defense. One day when teaching my Peaceful Self Defense System class, a young woman was asking what she could do about an abusive husband who got drunk and beat her. Before I could respond, an older lady sprang up, spoke in a booming voice and said, "Honey, I've been married twenty-three years. During the first week of our marriage my husband hit me. When he went to bed and fell asleep I got the heavy iron skillet out and hit him in the head and he spent the next week in the hospital. I went to see him and explained that if he ever hit me again... anyway, he got the idea." She sat down and no one in that room doubted her word.

I do not recommend hitting someone with a skillet. It worked for one lady, but she got lucky. Her moxie act of violence could have escalated the conflict, gotten her killed, or put her in jail. She did not consider the nonviolent act of walking out the door and getting appropriate help. Most of us, to some extent, unmindfully allow ourselves to be victimized. This often takes the form of being the target of *ridicule* or other Social Weapons. If we let people get away with mistreating us then we, in essence, have given them 'squatter's rights' to continue their abusive behavior. If we do nothing to put a stop to their assaults, it encourages them to continue their attacks.

Ma and Pa Groceries

Ma and Pa were owners of the corner grocery store in my old neighborhood. They had been struggling for years trying to get out of debt. One of the reasons that Ma and Pa were having financial difficulties is that one of them failed to keep a careful eye on customer shoplifting. Pa did not want to make any of the customers feel uncomfortable. He would divert his eyes. He just assumed that a certain percentage of theft went with the territory of having a retail store. Even when Pa spotted someone stealing he failed to do anything that might deter this form of territorial aggression. Ma was more outspoken and diligent in uncovering store theft. The problem was that most of the thefts occurred when Ma left Pa alone at the store.

Over the years I had grown fond of Ma and Pa. One day Ma was complaining to me about how they might have to close the store because they were being

targeted by so many thieves. I went home that night
trying to think of a solution for their shoplifting problem.
The next day I told Ma that I had come up with a
solution that might work. I suggested they install
cameras and take pictures of actors pretending to be
thieves who are stealing from the store. Then I
suggested that they print the pictures with the following
caption: "DO YOU KNOW THIS PERSON? PLEASE
HELP US CATCH THIEVES SO WE CAN KEEP OUR
PRICES REASONABLE." I advised them to post the
pictures in a prominent location in the store. To my
surprise they followed my advice to the letter. Ma later
estimated that the camera and poster strategy ended up
preventing close to fifteen hundred dollars a month in
lost inventory.

169

The shoplifting at Ma and Pa's Groceries had grown progressively worse because Pa did nothing to prevent shoplifters from depleting their inventory. It was not until something significant was done to defend against the Social Weapon *rapid takeover* that Ma and Pa were able to reasonably protect their livelihood.

The Cluttered Office Credenza

Penelope and Diane shared an office in an insurance agency. They had been fighting for control of their office credenza for over a year. Diane decorated the credenza to create a pleasing work atmosphere and professional image. Before Penelope moved into the office, the credenza remained free of clutter. Diane said a well organized environment helped her think more clearly.

Penelope saw the credenza as an extension of her territory and was in the habit of leaving the credenza covered with her current and past projects. She would leave her purse, box of Kleenex, bicycle helmet, bills, paperwork, water bottle, and even articles of clothing on the credenza.

One day Penelope spilled her coffee all over the credenza and ended up having to clear off her belongings in order to clean up the mess. Diane gladly helped her move the stuff over to Penelope's work area. At that time they reached an agreement to keep the credenza clear. Diane was happy and felt better about Penelope.

The Drama of Reconciliation

In the 1980's social scientists discovered that domestic human aggression often occurs with the purpose of gaining attention, with the intent of strengthening relationships. They learned that human aggression is often followed by what was thought to be a solely human act of reconciliation. In later years, animal experts showed that reconciliation is not solely a human act, since chimpanzees have been documented to make up after violent confrontations. Trying to make amends during the heat of battle doesn't work. Most chimpanzees seem to agree with me on this point.

Much fighting is for no reason at all. We get bored at times and make trouble in order to stimulate ourselves with drama. Later we find ourselves going through the drama of making up.

Territorial Defense

Our first line of defense is clearly marked boundaries. Boundaries show ownership. Often this is enough to stop people's aggression. We must defend what we feel we own. When boundaries are crossed we need to tell people. Our second line of defense is warning a person that they have crossed a territorial boundary. Peaceful Self Defense System students learn that responses to aggression must be direct and specific to the area under attack. If our defense is vague we will quickly see Social Weapons undermining us as we become angry, afraid and confused. Invaders need to be told where they stepped into our territory and they need to be told we want them out. Our third line of defense is the Peaceful Self Defense System explained in the third part of this book.

On War

In 1793, a twelve-year-old Prussian lance corporal named Carl Von Clausewitz began 23 years of fighting in wars against the French. Clausewitz rose to the rank of major-general and after his death his unfinished book *On War* was published. This book covers the way power, politics, and morality govern warfare. It is considered by most military theorists to be a classic for understanding warfare.

The more we remain emotionally unfazed by Social Weapons, the more power we hold for defending against them. Clausewitz wrote that defense can be a stronger form of war than attack. His concept of defense is to anticipate and be in the best position possible to parry attacks. Clausewitz maintains this preparedness is the only feature that turns an action into a defensive one.

He claims that countering aggression is what distinguishes defense from attack.

> *It is easier to hold ground than take it. It follows that defense is easier than attack, assuming both sides have equal means.*
>
> **Carl Von Clausewitz**
> *On War*

If we are attacked with Social Weapons and react against the assault by using similar Social Weapons, we have instantly moved from defense to attack. The act of being in attack mode transforms our defensive power into an offensive power that can hinder our chances for creating peace.

> *Invincibility lies in the defense; the possibility of victory in the attack.*
>
> **Sun Tzu**
> *The Art of War*

The anthropologist and behavioral scientist Robert Ardrey suggested that most members of the animal kingdom who defend territory acquire a home field advantage over attackers. It is not uncommon for us to develop a righteous indignation when our more personal territory is under attack. Our heightened concern for things dear to us can motivate us to explore our options for advantageous defense.

Thus far we have explained how being able to identify Social Weapons and understand territoriality gives us an advantage. When we fail to respond to aggression based on this understanding, we become hostile.

Hostility

All of us have behaved in a hostile manner at one time or another. Hostility likes to rear its miserable head when we are unable to defend against the aggression of another person. Hostility in the territorial model is an emotionally driven behavior. It is a retaliatory response that is usually aimed at the aggressor. When we really lose control we might take our hostility out on an innocent party or ourselves. We keep revisiting the scene of being wronged to justify our hostility.

When we become hostile we do not directly defend against aggression, but instead lash out in ways that might harm the aggressor, the territory, ourselves, or others around us. Common forms of hostility include self-defeating thought patterns, character assassination, gossip, backbiting, destruction of territory, and other ways of evening the score.

Beautiful Hawaiian Vacation

Years ago at the San Francisco Airport there was a guy in line in front of me checking in his bags with a Skycap. The traveler barked orders, insulting the Skycap and talking down to him. After the rude guy left, I said to the Skycap, "That guy was sure a jerk. How do you put up with people like him?" The Skycap said with a big smile, "By giving his luggage special attention. He is on the way to St. Louis, but his bags are taking a beautiful Hawaiian vacation."

Rather than being a form of aggression, it is quite the opposite of it. Hostility is retaliatory in nature.

Cornelis Bakker, M.D.
Marianne Bakker-Rabdau
No Trespassing!: Explorations
in Human Territoriality

The Bird

Laura Hillenbrand's book *Unbroken* is a World War II survival epoch about Louie Zamperini, the Olympic runner whom experts predicted would be the first person to break the four minute mile barrier. Rather than running his way into the history books, Louie fought in World War II. He was the bombardier on a B-24 Liberator that crashed into the Pacific Ocean. After the aircraft sunk, Louie survived two months in a raft that floated two thousand miles with grossly inadequate provisions. He eventually was captured by the Japanese and was forced to suffer in prison camps.

The American prisoners gave the Japanese guards nicknames. The most hated of the guards was a psychopath nicknamed 'The Bird'. The Bird beat Louie close to death on many occasions. In the camps Louie was able to survive only by refusing to give up. After the war his stubborn mind refused to give up the image of the Bird. His tormented thoughts of revenge led him down the path of alcohol abuse. This strategy at times blurred his thoughts but did little to extricate him from his former oppressor. Louie's postwar self-destructive behavior continued until he finally was able to free himself from his bonds of hostility by forgiving the Bird. This allowed him to quit alcohol. His need for retribution had caused him to harm himself and those dear to him.

Laura Hillenbrand's depiction of Louie's hostility is described in the following excerpt from her book, *Unbroken*.

> *The paradox of vengefulness is that it makes men dependent upon those who have harmed them, believing that their release from pain will come only when they make their tormentors suffer. In seeking the Bird's death to free himself, Louie had chained himself, once again, to the tyrant. During the war, the Bird had been unwilling to let go of Louie; after the war, Louie was unable to let go of the Bird.*

When we are unable to adequately defend territory that is important to us, hostility is a predictable response. If we are unable to fix our own hostile behavior, we become miserable. In this type of situation, we are usually using Social Weapons against ourselves. We might berate ourselves with thoughts like, "I could have acted different or done something better at the time of the attack." Often we just play the helpless victim. We use the Social Weapon *helplessness* on ourselves when we go around telling everyone except the transgressor how we were mistreated.

A Dozen Eggs

I was presenting the concept of hostility in a seminar when a woman in the audience raised her hand to ask a question. I called on her and she said, "I think I get this. Here's what happened. Is this hostility? Last week I went to the mall and drove around for twenty minutes looking for a parking place. The parking lot was packed and I finally saw an open spot to park." The woman became intense as she further described what happened. "I was getting ready to pull into the space when a guy in a shiny Corvette sped up, cut me off, and shot into the parking place. I rolled down the window and told him I was there first. He ignored me, jumped out of his car, and went on his way. I was furious and I wasn't about to let him get away with it. I bought a dozen eggs at the Seven-Eleven. I went back to the parking lot and splashed the eggs all over his car. It was a hot afternoon and the eggs dried real fast."

The woman smiled in satisfaction and said, "I
decided not to shop because I was so pissed off. I ended
up going home. Since then all I've thought about was
how that bastard deserved what he got. Is this what you
mean when you talk about hostility?" I answered, "You
have captured the idea. The sports car driver used the
Social Weapon *rapid takeover* on you. You became
angry and emotionally reacted to his use of a Social
Weapon with hostile behavior. In the territorial model,
hostility isn't a feeling. It's a behavior. The repetitive
mental chewing of past conflict is typical hostile
behavior."

The reason the woman became hostile was she had been unable to prevent her claimed territory from being taken over. After being disregarded and upstaged, she angrily tried to get even. The retribution came in the form of *rapid takeover* as she decorated the sports car with eggs. When we defend against aggression by using aggression, we escalate hostile behavior. More often than not, hostile behavior is destructive.

The behavior of conflicting participants becomes more understandable once we realize that human actions are governed by territorial needs and constraints.

A theory may be considered as a way of binding together a multitude of facts so that one may comprehend them all at once.

George Kelly
A Theory of Personality

Chapter 24

THREE ESSENTIAL HUMAN NEEDS

After forty years of working as a clinician, management consultant, organizational development specialist, and having taught thousands of seminars to help people get along, I repeatedly get asked the same basic question: "Why am I being treated like this?" To understanding this, we need to be able to grasp how hostility works and how we are affected by our requirements to have an identity, to be stimulated, and to feel secure. During most of our lifetimes, we operate without awareness of our essential psychological needs. Territorial behavior is strongly influenced by man's need for identity, stimulation, and security.

Carmine has an Affair

Carmine was a retired professional basketball player. She arrived at a health cafe after a long bike ride that took her to a trendy section of San Diego. She was seated next to Luther at the juice bar who was extremely tall and dressed in his gym clothes. Both of them were there to take a break from their bike rides. They talked and were instantly physically attracted to one another. She was excited that they shared so much in common. They decided to meet again the next day. They met at the cafe and got to know each other a little better.

Luther was married. Carmine was single and did not want to commit to a relationship that would limit her freedom. She thought a love affair would be fun if Luther could handle it. That ended up happening and along the way she fell in love.

Their amorous adventures lasted close to a year. When Carmine came to see me for counseling she recalled how she had first fallen head over heels in love. All she wanted to know was why she was being rejected. She said, "Luther always said he really loved me, too." Fighting back her tears, she said, "He was planning to leave his wife way before he met me. He said he was waiting for a big horse sale to happen so we could move in together. Why would he stay with a woman who has always been so hateful to him?" After asking Carmine a few questions, I learned that Luther's wife was independently wealthy. Carmine said, "Luther had a huge country estate, race horses, and a fancy sports car, but I guess it was his wife who owned it all."

I told Carmine, "The answer to your question can be found by looking at the three basic human needs. Like everyone, Luther needed to have an identity, be stimulated, and feel secure. These inherent needs are best understood in terms of their opposite definitions. The most basic need is for identity. Its opposite is anonymity. The need for identity is followed closely by the need for stimulation. Its opposite is boredom. The third need is more distant, but still powerful; and it is the need for security. Its opposite is anxiety. A real problem for people is that security is the birthplace of boredom and maybe that is what led you two to get together in the first place."

The affair was stimulating and fun for Carmine and Luther. But when he discovered his wife suspected that he might be seeing someone, it really kicked in his security needs. He began acting paranoid and nervous for several weeks before their break up. I told Carmine that Luther's identity had been threatened. I explained that identity is all about status, and how status drives primate behavior. Luther was risking his estate, race horses, sports car, and reputation. As Luther's current status with his family and friends became jeopardized, the security of being devoted to his wife became far more important than his need for outside stimulation.

As Carmine viewed the situation in context of the three innate needs, she was better able to understand the forces that drove Luther and was finally able to get over him. Carmine later told me that the perspective of looking at things from a needs standpoint helped her reconcile what took place.

The need for status (identity) has been regularly observed in all primates. Our need to have our perceived social status respected often sets us up for emotional letdowns. When the picture we have created of ourselves is defaced by another, we can expect to react with hostility.

When we are gossiping, putting someone else down, or complaining about our situation, we are often reacting out of boredom. We can feel justified using Social Weapons on others and at the same time find it stimulating. It is common to experience a certain satisfaction in using these weapons against others. But if we are caught ridiculing our boss, then we are in danger of becoming unemployed. In many similar situations, when we step over the line, we become subject to anxiety and insecurity. Once we realize our actions have put us in a precarious position, our need for security will supplant our need for stimulation. Most of the time, we are unaware of switching from one human need to the other.

Another Day at the IRS

An IRS investigator, Roy, met me at my office. It had nothing to do with my taxes as he came to me for personal guidance. He was having problems dealing with his boss, Hank. Hank would call Roy in for a meeting and then proceed to make numerous phone calls while ignoring Roy for long periods of time. After several months of being Hank's captive audience, Roy decided enough was enough. Roy had been employed by the IRS for twelve years and felt he deserved better. "Why am I being treated like this?" he asked. I explained to him the three innate human needs and gave him a strategy to rob Hank of getting his stimulation at Roy's expense.

The next time Roy was called into a meeting with Hank, I told him to take some of his office work to Hank's office. I instructed Roy to focus on his own projects when Hank was occupied on the phone. However, Roy was to give his undivided attention, remain courteous and respectful anytime Hank addressed him. During his next meeting, Roy continued with his own work, completely ignoring Hank when Hank was engrossed on the phone. Roy reported, "Hank was ill at ease that I worked while he chatted on the phone." When Hank saw Roy focusing on his own tasks, no longer being annoyed, and exhibiting no hostile behavior, the talking on the phone stopped and future meetings took place with minimal interruption. Roy robbed his boss of being stimulated at his expense. Hank was deprived of being able to enjoy his superior status over Roy.

Awareness of the human need for identity, stimulation, and security gives us an insight into behavior. I instruct my students to identify these three human needs when feeling threatened. This realization helps them make sense of why they felt victimized. Most of us feel more at ease once we understand the motivation behind people's inconsiderate behavior.

The true nature of things loves to hide and to stay hidden.

Heraclitus
Greek Philosopher

An understanding of how the territorial imperative drives our conduct helps us understand why we behave the way we do. In the next section, we will reveal the weapon-free skills and strategies we can use to successfully deal with contentious circumstances. Setting clear boundaries and having Peaceful Self Defense System skills to defend our territory greatly reduces conflict, hostility and stress.

PART THREE

PEACEFUL SELF DEFENSE SYSTEM SKILLS

Chapter 26

METHODS FOR CONTROLLING DRAMA

*By being aware of what's going
on in our situation, reaction time can be
increased by three hundred percent.*

National Geographic TV series
Fight Science

The Peaceful Self Defense System skills described in this section are used for defending territory, evaluating options, deciding the best course of action and getting the best outcome.

Situations will change, and the Social Weapons used against us will vary. In spite of that, the basic skills remain the same. They are designed to defend our territory.

A Dozen Core Skills

Our Peaceful Self Defense System is based on a dozen core skills. The skills are dynamic. They work in combination and compliment each other. The skills are:

1. Recognizing Irritation
2. Identifying our Issue of Concern
3. Sticking to the Issue
4. Bargaining
5. Remaining Courteous
6. The Warrior's Stance
7. Planning Strategy
8. Paying the Price
9. Handling Negative Emotions
10. Using Self-reinforcement
11. Practicing Delayed Mastery
12. Signaling Defensive Intent.

Chapter 27

SKILL # 1: RECOGNIZING IRRITATION

Irritation is like an alarm that sounds when our boundaries have been crossed. Feeling irritated is a signal to look for the cause of our upset.

High levels of irritation are easy to recognize. We can measure the level of our irritation on a scale of zero to ten. Zero would be no irritation. Ten is an unbearable amount of irritation. If a burglar breaks into our home, or our spouse confesses to an affair, or we get fired, our irritation level could be between a seven and a ten. We know we are upset.

At low levels, irritation is harder to recognize—the ones, twos, and threes. What often happens is that we minimize the irritation. We might think, "It's not that big a deal. I can live with it." Chronic irritations occur daily, yet most people let them go by unresolved. Exchanges with an unpleasant coworker, or put-downs from a friend can be brushed aside or ignored. While not every irritant is worthy of a response, we can eliminate many of them by using peaceful self defense skills to defend our boundaries.

Low level irritations are often ignored because we feel uncomfortable confronting others. We might also avoid taking defensive action because we don't want to pay the price of the time and effort it takes. Smaller irritants may show up as uncomfortable physical sensations, like a tight stomach, clamped jaw, tense neck, or clenched fists. These sensations are warning signals that our territory is being invaded.

By keeping track of what irritates us, and by successfully defending our boundaries, we reduce the buildup that causes the 'last straw' phenomenon. This refers to the Arabic proverb about a seemingly insignificant piece of straw that loaded a camel beyond its capacity and as a consequence broke its back.

It is wishful thinking to assume unpleasant attacks will stop just by ignoring them. When we disregard the ongoing build up of disturbing occurrences, we might unconsciously be using weapons against ourselves. We might be using the Social Weapons *helplessness* and *definition* when we think, "Oh, here I am being insulted again. I just don't have the energy to deal with this."

Some irritations recur in daily, weekly, monthly, or yearly cycles. Every year at Thanksgiving, a relative's obnoxious stories undermine an otherwise wonderful Thanksgiving dinner. Our spouses upset us by forgetting an anniversary or just being late to dinner. These irritations can consume us and take away some of our joy. Repeated irritations challenge our relationships to their breaking points.

Other people are not always the source of our irritation and pent up hostility. Sometimes we feel guilty for failing to do something. We become upset when we forget where we put our keys. We get discouraged with our lack of control when we eat too much or behave badly. An effective way to get in touch with our irritations is to keep an Irritation Log.

Below is a basic template for an Irritation Log. On the left side of the log there is an irritation thermometer that goes from a scale of zero to ten. Zero means a state of no irritation, while ten shows we have reached our limit. The bulb at the top of the scale has the word TILT written on it. Knowing what it takes for us to reach our boiling point can motivate us to take suitable action early on, and avoid contributing to our own emotional upheavals.

When using the irritation log we suggest writing the numerical level of irritation in the column closest to

IRRITATION LOG

Put 1-10	What Happened?	What Did you Do? Outcome?	Weapons Used?

(Left side scale: 10, 9, 8, 7, 6, 5, 4, 3, 2, 1 — labeled TILT at top)

the left side of the chart. The next column over is for explaining what happened. Let's use the example of the young lady who smashed eggs all over the man's shiny new Corvette. Under what happened she might write, "I went to the mall, found a parking space and was about to pull in when a man in a sports car cut me off and took my spot."

The next column is for explaining what we did about it. In our example the young lady might write, "I went to a convenience store, bought eggs, and smashed them all over his car." In that same column we are reminded to describe the outcome of the event. Again, the young lady might write, "Then I stewed about what a jerk he was for days." The last column is where we list the Social Weapons the invader(s) used against us. In the young lady's case she could write *rapid takeover.*

When we catch ourselves stewing over an earlier trespass of our boundaries, it is an ideal time to document our story in the irritation log. We might include how we felt about the situation and prepare ourselves for similar events in the future. Instead of using retaliatory weapons like the young lady did, we advocate use of peaceful skills whenever the opportunity presents itself. During one of my Peaceful Self Defense System workshops one of the students, Judy, filled out the log as follows:

In the first column of the log Judy wrote a "4" to rate her level of irritation.

In the second column for explaining what happened, Judy wrote, "My husband Tom likes to eat as soon as he comes home from work. I asked him to call me anytime he was going to come home late from work. I wanted to be informed of any changes in his schedule so I could time dinner with his arrival. Tom said he would, but a few days later, he forgot to tell me he was going to be late."

In the third column for describing what was done and the final outcome, Judy wrote, "After waiting for fifteen minutes, I covered both plates with tin foil and placed them in the oven to keep them warm. Tom arrived home thirty minutes late. He apologized for being late and for not calling to warn me. I told him I would only accept his apology if he would give me his solemn word that this would never happen again. I felt better after Tom promised to call me every workday sometime before 5:00 p.m. to tell me when he'd be home."

In the fourth column for listing the Social Weapons used, Judy wrote "*pretense* and *rapid takeover*".

Pretense was used against Judy when Tom did not honor his commitment to call her if he was going to be late for dinner. Judy recognized *rapid takeover* being used when Tom did not show up on time.

By keeping this log, we can identify patterns of irritation and be able to predict what will make us irritated and angry in the future. This knowledge allows us to anticipate and prevent situations and people from upsetting us. A common result of not dealing with irritation is increased hostility. Our hostile behavior can be harmful to us and everyone around us. Hostility is a practiced behavior that can become self defeating. By peacefully responding at the time of our initial irritation we can forgo getting even.

Chapter 28

SKILL #2: IDENTIFYING OUR ISSUE OF CONCERN

Identifying our Issue of Concern is the most important self defense skill. Most of the skills to follow depend on knowing just what we want. If a friend borrows money from us and doesn't return it, is the important issue the money, the friendship, the time it takes to get the money back, or all of these? In any moment of conflict, it is important to be able to identify exactly what we want from the situation. This is called our issue. To defend against Social Weapons we want to be direct and specific about our issue.

Identifying our Issue of Concern may seem simple, but that's not always the case. Often it is useful to identify what territory is involved. Remember the story "Lunch Litter?" At work Julia was assigned projects that required her constant use of a computer. Every day she would come back from lunch to find John using her computer and making a mess of her work area.

Julia told John she didn't like him using her computer when she was at lunch. John responded, "It's not yours, it belongs to the company." True, it wasn't Julia's property, but John's use of the computer interfered with her productivity at work. She was paid to be a project manager, not to spend time cleaning up

John's messes. Julia got her way by making interference with company productivity her issue.

We might ask ourselves, "Do we care about keeping all, some, or none of the territory?" Sometimes, this is difficult to decide quickly, yet people using Social Weapons may press us for an immediate response. If we aren't sure, our issue changes to buying time. Just say, "I want time to think about this." If the other party refuses to give us more time, then we might excuse ourselves, to go to a restroom or take a phone call. Once we have time to think, our main objective is being clear on our primary issue.

Chapter 29

SKILL # 3: STICKING TO THE ISSUE

Sticking to the Issue is an important skill, as we are constantly being distracted by Social Weapons and emotions that can make us forget what it is that we really want. Sometimes we feel satisfied when we reactively use Social Weapons to hurt the other party. Those combative licks typically compound conflict and make us forget what we are trying to achieve.

In the heat of battle it is easy to be led away from our goal. Humans have a tendency to deal with a variety of issues all at once. In casual conversation it's fine to shift from topic to topic, but not when our communication must accomplish a specific purpose. Remember, our issue is important mainly to us, not the other party. Two people in conflict with each other rarely agree on the importance of the other's issue.

Never Touch a Downed Power Line

One day while watching the local news during a windstorm I saw an episode with a supervising lineman giving advice to young children about downed power lines. He told the children there were five things they needed to remember if they saw a downed line. He said number one was, "Stay away from the downed line and don't touch it. Then he said, "Number two is if you see a downed power line stay away from it and don't touch it. Can you guess number three?" A few of the children responded, "Stay away from the line and don't touch it." "What about number four?" he asked. "Stay away from the line and don't touch it," all the children answered. And then he asked the children if they could guess what number five was. "Stay away from the line and don't touch it!" the children sang out.

The lineman made sure that his life-saving issue was taught through repetition.

Simple Broken Record Technique

Simple Broken Record is a technique that relies on repetition to keep the spotlight on an issue. Simple Broken Record is the restating and repeating of an issue just like the lineman did with the children. It is continued nonstop until we get our way or reach an acceptable compromise.

Taylor Swift

At the age of 10, a stockbroker's daughter named Taylor Swift fell in love with country music. Taylor is now a very successful songwriter, singer and musician. At 10, she begged her parents to take her to Nashville, the Mecca of country music. Taylor used Simple Broken Record. She told reporter Leslie Stahl during a 60 Minutes news interview that her repeats were on a loop: "Why don't we go to Nashville? Can we get a trip to Nashville? I looked up a tour brochure about Nashville. Can we go see Nashville?" By age eleven she was on her way to Nashville.

I Won't Pay a Cent More

A woman in one of my classes used Simple Broken Record to buy a used car at a reasonable price. Her husband went with her, but she made him promise not to talk and to act as if he had all the time in the world. Every time the salesman insisted that the car was worth more than she wanted to pay, she said, "I'll give you $5,000 for the car and I won't pay a cent more." After half an hour and two consultations with his manager, the salesman gave in.

The woman's straightforward use of Simple Broken Record worked because her relationship with the salesman meant very little to her. Whenever we simply repeat only our issue we are likely to cause the other party to feel frustrated, helpless, and angry. Simple Broken Record has its place, but when it is used without tact or concern for the other party it can undermine relationships.

Simple Broken Record must be used with care to keep the other party from feeling attacked. The following story shows this technique being used with little regard for others. It does, however, illustrate how Simple Broken Record can keep the spotlight on our issue.

Gloria Goes to the Emergency Room

Gloria came to my social work office at a medical center for her weekly counseling appointment. She was agitated and I asked what was wrong. She said, "On my way up here to see you I stopped at the emergency room to have my blood pressure checked and they refused. If I don't have it checked my daughter says I will die." I told Gloria she could get her blood pressure checked at the ER if she went about it by becoming a broken record.

When record players were popular, a broken record was one that stuck and would just keep repeating the same phrase. Gloria understood what I meant. I instructed her to go back to the emergency room with the task to see how many times she would have to repeat herself to get her blood pressure taken. I suggested that she began each sentence with the word 'I'. The instructions were that no matter what was said at the emergency room, Gloria was to say in response, "I want my blood pressure taken." I told her she would never make it to twenty repeats. Gloria said, "This won't work, they will think I'm nuts." I replied, "I bet you will get your blood pressure taken." Gloria departed for the ER and about fifteen minutes later she came back to the office with a big smile on her face. "How many times?" I asked. "Thirteen," she replied.

I don't normally recommend expensive use of the ER just to have your blood pressure checked. Gloria had psych problems and was a chronic ER over user. Once Gloria saw that Simple Broken Record got her what she wanted, she became empowered and was more confident. This led to her learning to use the appointment center and see her primary care doctor instead of using the ER.

Creative Broken Record Technique

Simple Broken Record requires very little thought. It is a powerful way to keep us on our issue but can be too blunt. Simple Broken Record is the forerunner of Creative Broken Record, which is more sophisticated. When using the Peaceful Self Defense System skills the magic word is 'AND.' Use of "and" instead of "but" helps us direct another's thought processes and avoid negative responses.

I learned how to use the magic word 'AND' when auditing a class from one of my instructors at the University of Washington's Department of Psychiatry. At that time, the department was very psychoanalytical in its view of human behavior. The class I audited was about the advantages of using the behavioral approach.

The psychoanalytic view is if you change the way you think and feel, your behavior will change. The behavioral approach is if you change your behavior, the way you think and feel will change. As a result, when the instructor taught psychiatry students, he anticipated that many of them would not agree with his point of view.

Sitting in and observing I began to see a very interesting phenomenon. A student began to argue with the instructor that analytic, not behavioral theory was more useful. The instructor looked at the student with great attentiveness until he had finished, then said, "Yes, your point of view is well-founded. Analytic theory definitely can lead to greater insight." The student nodded in agreement.

After the instructor achieved this nodding effect, he continued by saying "AND, I believe that certain behavioral approaches have the capacity to produce a desired effect when dealing with common neuroses." The student was now considering the efficacy of using behavioral techniques. I could see that the instructor held the student's interest and was able to easily overcome his argument.

After the class I asked the instructor how he could so easily get back on track and keep people with contrary opinions listening to him. He replied, "I just try to remain friendly and use the magic word AND." The instructor went on to explain, "The words 'but' or 'however' cause the conflicting party to become defensive. Instead of listening, the person begins to think about what he wants to say next." Combining this technique with Simple Broken Record gave birth to a more refined technique, Creative Broken Record.

Opponents confront us continually, but actually there is no opponent there. Enter deeply into an attack and neutralize it as you draw that misdirected force into your own sphere.

Morihei Ueshiba
The Art of Peace

When she used Simple Broken Record, Gloria disregarded anything the ER nurse had to say while she continued to repeat that she wanted her blood pressure taken. This repetitive ploy by itself does not build good will. Creative Broken Record, on the other hand, takes others' feelings into account. By treating others well, we are more likely to be treated kindly.

The creative part of this technique is our show of respect by demonstrating we have been good listeners. We want to make the speaker feel heard by looking attentive, paraphrasing key points that were made before we return to our issue. Other listening tips are: avoid interrupting, maintain friendly eye contact, give an air of having all the time in the world to listen, and use non-verbal gestures such as nodding.

Our nodding can become contagious. When I was a child my great aunt had a drinking bird made of wood that sat on the edge of a glass of water. I use to give it a little push on the back of its head and to my delight it would continue to bob up and down. Once we get the other party nodding like a drinking bird it is time to use the magic word 'AND' and then state our issue. Our statement should begin with the word 'I' and then say what we want or don't want. An 'I' statement refrains from using the word 'you' which the other party may hear as labeling and thus become defensive.

Remember to avoid using the words 'but' and 'however' to link our creative statement with our issue.

Careful listening is necessary if we want to be listened to in return. Sometimes we have to force ourselves to give our full attention to the other person. This requires being mindfully present. Creative Broken Record relies on the use of active listening and acknowledging the other's feelings. The paraphrasing of what we have heard also gives us more time to prepare a response.

Patience is necessary to make Creative Broken Record work. Encounters often take longer than we expect. Creative Broken Record is not a technique we can hurry our way through. By preparing ourselves to spend plenty of time it becomes easier for us to remain calm and kind to the other party. If we are pressed for time our impatience decreases our chance of success.

Nature has given to man one tongue,
but two ears, that we may hear from
others twice as much as we speak.

Epicetus
Greek philosopher

Walkup Window

Back in the 1970s, banks were beginning to offer their customers drive-through banking. At that time, I was courting my wife Emi. One Friday at 4:45 p.m. I arrived home on the train with my paycheck in hand. I needed cash to take Emi on a date. I ran to my bank which was just behind my house. The bank had been closed since 3:00 p.m. but the drive-through window was still open. Automatic teller machines didn't exist in those days. I felt foolish as I stood in line behind the last car but I didn't want to waste time getting my car out of the garage just to drive across the street.

When my turn came, the teller said, "I'm sorry, but you have to be in a car to cash a check." I replied in a friendly tone, "I understand that it's necessary to be in a car, AND I would really like to have my check cashed." The teller said, "I'm sorry sir, but insurance regulations prevent us from cashing checks for people who are not in their cars." I persisted, "I understand that you can't help me because of insurance reasons, AND I would really like to have my check cashed."

Not knowing what to do, the teller consulted her coworker at the other window, and then turned back to me. "No, we can't help you if you are not in a car." Seeing that the teller was using the Social Weapon *helplessness*, I said, "I understand that it's impossible and you can't help me AND it's very important for me to have my check cashed. If you were in my position, what would you do?" The teller said, "Well, I would talk to the manager, Mr. Johnson." Standing firmly in my spot, I asked her politely to get him.

Just before Mr. Johnson arrived, the woman in the car behind me stuck her head out the window and said, "Hey, you're welcome to get in my car so you can cash your check." I laughed, thanked her and said, "No, I hope to have it taken care of in just a minute. If not I'll gladly take you up on your offer."

Mr. Johnson listened to my request and stated, "I'm sorry, but our insurance regulations won't allow us to cash a check unless you are in a car." Undaunted by this wall of *helplessness*, I courteously said, "I understand that you need to comply with insurance regulations." Mr. Johnson nodded his head and smiled and seemed happy to be understood. That was my cue to seize the moment and I did so by saying, "AND it's critical for me to get this check cashed today."

I was surprised when Mr. Johnson turned to the teller and told her to cash my check as I was expecting to have to continue using the technique Creative Broken Record. I thanked Mr. Johnson, assuring him that I would not walk through the drive-through line again. He smiled and said, "You should be glad to hear that in two weeks we're going to add walkup windows."

During the entire walkthrough encounter I remained calm, collected and respectful because I knew that would increase my chances of getting the check cashed. I paraphrased everything the teller said and always added, "AND I would like my check cashed." I used time as an ally to defend against *helplessness*. A bureaucratic form of *helplessness* is the most common weapon used by employees charged with enforcing the rules. After getting what I wanted, I then apologized to the person in line behind me for the delay I caused.

This check-cashing problem was quickly resolved. I stuck to my issue using the Creative Broken Record technique. By carefully repeating what was said to me, I demonstrated to the bank employees that I was respectfully listening to them. After paraphrasing the employees' statements, I used the magic word 'AND' before restating my issue. By remaining patient, I was able to get what I wanted without ramping up conflict.

Regular practice of Creative Broken Record helps prepare us for times when it is challenging to stick to an issue. With practice the technique can be used with enough skill to hide the fact that we are using a set protocol to get heard. We simply remain calm and repeat our issue after we enthusiastically preface it with a friendly statement that shows we have been listening to the other party's point of view. After all, Dale Carnegie made millions telling people how to win friends and influence people through friendly enthusiasm.

Defective Shirt

Charles was practicing the Peaceful Self Defense System. He was seeking a refund at a department store. He showed the salesclerk his defective shirt. The shirt was purchased a month before and was never worn. The clerk said, "I'm sorry, but we don't give refunds unless the merchandise is returned within two weeks of purchase. Charles said, "I can understand that you have a policy of not giving refunds after two weeks (this showed he was listening), AND since the shirt was unknowingly bought with a defect and has remained unused I would really appreciate a refund." Charles was surprised to get his way in less than five minutes of his time.

Rip-off Campaign

In the 1980's I worked at a neurosurgery center. I used Creative Broken Record to defend my position with an administrator named Dave. He was not my boss, but was higher ranked than I was in the organization. I had been directed to run the company program to raise funds for a well-known charity. All of the managers and administrators were expected to support this charitable campaign. When I gave a presentation explaining our company's fund-raising drive at a staff meeting, Dave interrupted me before I was finished by saying that the charity was a rip-off. He complained that too much money was swallowed up in administrative costs while a very small percentage of the proceeds reached the people who needed it.

I was surprised at this high-ranking administrator's show of disrespect for company policy and miffed at having my presentation undermined. I said nothing to Dave at the meeting because it is more difficult to get someone to compromise his 'truth' in front of an audience. I went directly to his office afterward to explain my issue: In the future I expected him to support my efforts on behalf of the charity.

Dave became defensive and started telling me what was wrong with the charity. I listened attentively and said I understood his point of view that the charitable organization pays too much in overhead and not enough money goes to the cause. I said that in the future I wanted his support whenever I presented the program. He continued to be defensive and I continued to listen to him and repeat my issue. I told him that everything he said about the charity might well be true, and it had been chosen by management, and reiterated my issue. In the future I wanted his support anytime I presented the program. Finally he admitted he was remiss for failing to toe the company line and that in the future he would not undermine my efforts.

Experiences like these have taught me that the more time we invest in listening to the other person, the more we increase our chances of being heard. We don't mean listening with a blank expression. We mean making an effort to be interested, enthusiastic, agreeable, and friendly. This will cause the other person to be more interested in what we have to say. The more we listen, and the more kind and enthusiastic we are about the other's point of view, the faster we will get our own point across.

The dialogue I had with Dave is an example of Creative Broken Record being used to get an issue resolved:

"Hi Dave. Do you have a moment to talk to me?"

"Sure Chris. Come on in."

"I want to talk to you about the meeting."

"Didn't I make my opinion clear enough?"

"Dave I sympathize with everything you said AND I would really like your support when I have to run one of the meetings."

"Why in the world would I want to back your shameless charity? It only exists to benefit some greedy businessmen."

"You know Dave, I have no doubt in my mind that you do not trust this charity and I do not disagree with you. It was a real unpleasant surprise when I found out that I was picked to run this company fundraiser. I also have misgivings regarding this charity AND I would really like your support when I have to direct one of the meetings."

"Look Chris, you know as well as I do most of the money we are raising is going to the wrong people. All I was doing was giving my opinion. Someone around here has to speak up."

"You know Dave, I really respect your opinion, and I know in the charities too much money often goes to the wrong people, AND I would really like your support when I have to run one of the meetings."

"Come on Chris. It is really a stretch for me to support something that I don't believe in and I think you are overreaching your authority to come into my office and try to pressure me to support this unworthy charity."

"Dave, the last thing I want to do in this world is to overreach my authority and I would never want to pressure you to conform with upper management's favorite philanthropic projects AND I would really like your support when I have to run one of the meetings."

"OK Chris, I see that you are in a position not of your choosing and I'll try to avoid undermining the company's project in the future."

"Thank you for your time and listening to me. I really appreciate your support."

Once I realized that Dave was going to comply with my issue I stopped using Creative Broken Record. Often we are tempted to push the other person until we receive an apology. During the conversation with Dave I deliberately kept the tone of my voice friendly and controlled my body language so I would be perceived as agreeable. Once I felt Dave understood my issue I refrained from asking for more.

Dave might have felt alarmed when I mentioned that it was upper management's fundraiser. It could have occurred to him that he was now subject to anyone at the meeting blowing the whistle regarding his sabotaging the CEO's directives. My intention was not to use threatening Social Weapons like *over the barrel* which is why I chose to have our discussion take place in Dave's private office. If what was said had taken place in front of an audience, it would have come across more intimidating and personal than intended.

Cruel Remarks

Suzy was a student in nursing school. The three girls who sat behind her would spend class time annoying her with cruel remarks. They would say things like, "Her questions are dumb, her hair looks awful, and she is not going to make it through school." Suzy complained to the teacher, but nothing changed. The teacher's failure to confront the girls caused Suzy to become more determined to end this cycle of being abused. After attending a Peaceful Self Defense System seminar, Suzy worked on her delivery of Creative Broken Record until she felt absolutely prepared to tackle the problem. She was actually looking forward to absorbing the assault and repeating her issue in front of the entire class.

At the beginning of the next class Suzy raised her hand and asked a question. Instantly one of Suzy's tormentors loudly said to her two friends, "There she goes with another dumb question." Suzy turned around and faced the three girls and calmly stated, "I understand you think my question was dumb AND I would really appreciate it if you would stop putting me down." She reported that the three were quiet for the rest of the class.

Our minds can easily become overtaxed when trying to cope with multiple challenges at the same time. When we are stressed and unclear about what to do or say next, time seems to speed up as we experience our minds uncontrollably shifting in panic from one possible solution to the next.

You have to run fast to stay where you are when the ground is moving under your feet.

Louis Carroll
Alice's Adventures In Wonderland

To lessen our mental pressure it is important to narrow down the important issues during a conflict and focus on dealing with one issue at a time. Suzy decided that her issue was that she felt she was being abused. She could have made the mistake of arguing about details of the many insulting attacks she had suffered. Instead Suzy's recipe for success was not to be in a hurry while neutrally restating the insulters' opinions and continuing to state her issue. Knowing what she was going to say next made her feel confident and unpressured.

Remaining calm, friendly, and courteous while avoiding Social Weapons makes it easier to be heard. For example, if someone says, "You are way too sensitive about being overweight for someone not willing to do something about it," you could reply, "I appreciate your concern, I tend to agree with you that I'm way too sensitive when it comes to talking about my weight, AND I would really be grateful if we could avoid talking about my weight in the future." This tactic acknowledges the role of our own feelings in order to have our issue heard.

Dealing with Bureaucratic Helplessness

We have a better chance of succeeding with business or government bureaucrats when we avoid becoming rushed due to time restraints. The Peaceful Self Defense System skills are difficult to use when we feel pressed for time. Fulfillment tends to be unobtainable when we appear in a hurry. Conveying the message that we are rooted to the ground and have all the time in the world helps us combat the weapon *helplessness*. This can work even when we are on the phone. Keeping our focus on Remaining Kind and Courteous while using Creative Broken Record can help us maintain this unhurried state of mine.

When we remain relaxed and kind it becomes difficult for an agent to dismiss our needs. We increase our chances of getting what we want by demonstrating to the other party that his message is being heard. We are not going to get anywhere with our agenda until the bureaucratic stance is addressed. A common reason for things going awry is our failing to confirm that we understand the other's point of view. This view could be their stated inability to help us. When we stop being courteous with our listening we give the other party a reason to be unkind back to us. By restating their company policy we show that we understand what we are being told. Being friendly throughout the process is the most important factor in getting help.

Chapter 30

SKILL # 4: BARGAINING

Being willing and able to bargain is critical for maintaining personal relationships. Bargaining can help us build a reputation as a reasonable person to deal with. In many situations, remaining peaceful and Sticking to the Issue will naturally lead to Bargaining.

The Meatball Sandwich

The following story is from a police report in the Tacoma News Tribune, March 28th, 1991, by Jerry Holloron. A robbery started when a customer walked into a Subway shop about 4:45 p.m. Monday and ordered a meatball sandwich. As a clerk waited to take his money, the customer-turned-robber pulled out a revolver and announced, "By the way, this is a holdup." The manager asked the man what he wanted. The robber said he wanted all the money - and negotiations began. The manager asked the robber if he would accept $10 and the sandwich. The robber replied that he would take no less than $20 and the sandwich. The deal was done and the robber fled in a getaway car.

Battle of The Break Room

Fred worked at a plastic coating company. The most disagreeable thing about work was dealing with his self-absorbed manager. When the workers were in the break room for lunch, the manager had the habit of heating up his tuna fish sandwich in the microwave. The smell was unbearable to several of the workers. They asked the manager if there was any chance he could stop smelling up the break room. The manager told them they would just have to live with it. Because of the manager's unwillingness to bargain, the workers quit using the break room.

One day Tom, the regional Vice President, was giving a tour of the facilities to a potential client. To Tom's dismay, many of the work stations looked very unprofessional with foodstuff and their containers scattered around. After Tom made his sales presentation, he made a beeline to the manager's office.

When Tom arrived at the office he found it empty. He searched the facilities for the manager until he found him in the break room. The aroma of microwaved tuna fish sandwiches caused Tom to step back in revulsion. Tom reminded the manager that it was his job to make sure the workers do all they could to keep the facilities looking like a showroom. He stated, "If I ever see this place looking like this again, I'm going make sure you get fired."

The manager quickly arranged a meeting with the workers and discovered that the reason they were eating at their work stations was because of his refusal to quit smelling up the break room. The workers were unified. They stuck to their issue by saying that the smell forced them to eat elsewhere. The final result of their Bargaining was that all parties agreed to resume using the break room as long as the manager took his tuna somewhere else.

A Room Full Of Conflict

When I teach the Peaceful Self Defense System class and finish talking about Creative Broken Record, I ask the students to play a game. Each class member is to pick a partner. These partners become a pair and each pair is assigned a number of one or two. Number one is told that he has 'it,' and number two wants 'it'. 'It' is not to be turned into a person, place, or thing.

Number one is told to keep 'it' by using Social Weapons. Number two is told to go after 'it' using Social Weapons. I give the class some examples of Social Weapon use. "Do you care about me at all?" *(guilt)*. "Why are you being so uptight about this?" (combination of *psychoanalysis* and *ridicule*). "If you just let me hold it, I will give it right back" (possible *rapid takeover)*. "You know I have a short period of time to live and you don't care at all about me" *(guilt* and possible *counterfeit illness*). I then say go and each

219

pair begins to use their Social Weapons to get 'it' or to keep 'it.' The room instantly turns into a madhouse. Everyone is screaming, using Social Weapons, making threats, or just grabbing 'it.' Finally, I yell "Stop!"

After the participants laugh and calm down, I announce, "Now, number one wants 'it' and number two has 'it.' This time number one can use Social Weapons and number two can only respond with Creative Broken Record." Someone usually asks, "Isn't number one at an advantage getting to use Social Weapons?" I always reply, "No. Number one does not have the advantage when number two uses Creative Broken Record and remains focused on the issue." "Go!" I shout. The participants are this time in a semi-uproar, but not as crazy as the first round. "Stop!" I again yell.

Then I ask, "Ready for round three?" and announce, "This time number one is to use only Creative Broken Record and number two is to use only Creative Broken Record. If I catch anyone using Social Weapons, your game is over. Number one will start by saying, 'I understand that you want to keep it and I want you to give it to me.' Number two will reply with, 'I understand that you want me to give it to you and I want to keep it.' Remember not to use any weapons. Is everyone ready? Go!" Many games end quickly as people fall right into Social Weapon use. Those who stay with the exercise and use no Social Weapons find that without even trying they begin Bargaining for whatever the 'it' is.

When two people communicate directly and ask for exactly what they want, Bargaining is a natural outcome. Social Weapon use keeps drama, manipulation, and emotional reactivity in high gear and bargains are rarely achieved. Dr. Cornelis Bakker used to say, "If you just ask for what you want, you will be surprised how often you get it."

Bargaining

The goal of Bargaining is to reach a compromise that reduces conflict. In order to reach an agreement, all parties need to be willing to give up something. Neither party will get everything they want.

There are two basic types of Bargaining:
1) An exchange of territory and
2) A division of territory.

Commerce is an exchange of territory. We exchange money for goods or services. In our personal life, we exchange responsibilities or do one another reciprocal favors such as household chores. The request is, "You do this for me and I will do that for you."

Bargaining can be an exchange of possessions. For example, during a divorce one partner could say, "How about you getting the sports car and I get the boat?" In divisions of territory, parties agree on what they feel is a fair distribution of a single item. If three people are dividing up a pizza with four slices, they might agree that the fourth slice can be cut into three sections.

Bargaining might involve two people wanting to watch different television shows that are aired at the same time. The compromise could be to record one of the shows while the other one is being watched. If the technology is not available for them to record, a different bargain might be made. Perhaps the solution ends up being that one gets the rest of the ice cream and the other gets to choose the program.

It makes sense to be happy, not dismayed, when someone wants something from us. This puts us in a good negotiating position. It is an opportunity to ask for something we want from the other person in exchange.

If we suggest a proposal that is unfavorable to another party it would be unrealistic to expect them to agree to it. However, it might be acceptable for a husband to bargain with his wife to accompany him to a party she does not want to go to if he agrees to go to her nephew's circumcision ceremony. Neither party might be thrilled about what they have to give up. But, they might be satisfied in knowing they are getting something they want.

Hidden agendas make compromise difficult. While working as a clinical therapist, I counseled a mother and daughter about a dispute over the family car.

I found out the mother knew exactly what would happen if her daughter got the car. She would drive off to see her boyfriend. The mother did not like her daughter's boyfriend and suspected that he was a drug dealer. The daughter also knew what would happen if she got the car. She would drive right off to see her boyfriend. I directed the discussion to their real issue. They needed to come to terms over the issue of seeing the boyfriend.

To find success while Bargaining, it is important to make all issues explicit. Within minutes, people tend to remember things very differently. We need to spell out details when we iron out an agreement. To avoid future squabbles and keep the terms clear, we would do well to put the terms down in writing and have all parties sign it. When the other parties refuse to sign the terms of what was agreed upon, their signing it becomes our issue. If they are still not willing to sign then we cannot count on any follow through with the agreement. One course of action would be to have them read the written agreement and verbally give it their okay and leave them a copy. That would increase their chances of complying.

When we are worried about someone's faulty memory or misinterpretation it pays to write the agreement with a way out. A good safety valve when making a bargain is the use of a time limit. For example, "Let's try this for two weeks to see how it is works for us. It has to make sense for you and me. Can we meet a week from Sunday to make sure we are both still happy with this arrangement?" If both parties agree to a trial period, it should also be in the written agreement.

If there is not enough time to resolve our issue, setting a new appointment becomes the issue. We might say, "Sorry, I'm late to another appointment and have to stop now. I would really like to work out an agreement with you that benefits both of us. When can we get together?"

While negotiating, it is important to remain calm and courteous throughout the process. Often we feel the allure of using Social Weapons. This urge must be suppressed in order to achieve a peaceful outcome.

Solid bargains with family, friends, and coworkers make life far less stressful. We begin to understand the character of people when we observe how well they keep their end of a bargain.

The formal process of mediation provides a useful forum for cheater detection.

Richard Coniff
The Ape In The Corner Office

Chapter 31

SKILL # 5: REMAINING KIND AND COURTEOUS

Remaining Kind and Courteous is a must for reducing conflict. Peaceful behavior allows us to stay on our issue by keeping negative emotions from taking over the conversation. Civility given is often reciprocated.

Being disrespectful is a sure fire way to create an adversarial situation. When we treat people poorly, we encourage more conflict. Being mean and rude creates hard feelings.

Remaining Kind and Courteous helps create a peaceful environment that supports being heard. Keeping conversation calm and friendly makes it likely the other party will listen to our issue. When we practice kindness and courtesy during an upset, we increase the chances of getting our way. Our goal is to create a setting conducive to friendly communication. Kindness and courtesy are contagious ingredients that foster cooperation and goodwill.

Our congenial behavior is directly observable to the other party. It is especially important to make sure we abstain from using *ridicule* or other Social Weapons. By self-monitoring our behavior with an emphasis on displaying a tranquil and pleasant demeanor, we increase our chances of keeping things civil. Also, being in a hurry can seem rude. To avoid this unwanted perception, we let the other party talk as we focus on patiently listening to what is being said. We do all we can to let them know we are listening and understand. To accomplish this we avoid talking over the other person. In creating a friendly scenario, it is advantageous for us to refrain from interrupting the other party's train of thought.

When the other person is talking, it is counterproductive to make impatient gestures or sighs. During a serious discussion we can wear a serious expression, but we want friendliness to shine though. Unflattering comments or name calling generally cause negative emotional reactions. Our issue becomes lost when the other person feels under attack. Other behaviors that lead to unwanted consequences are using an unfriendly tone of voice or threatening body language. This unwanted body language includes advancing into the other person's personal space, hovering, fidgeting or showing any signs of not paying attention.

All of us have made impolite comments like, "What are you yapping about now? Can't you see I'm busy? That is the stupidest thing I've ever heard." It is better to appear caring by politely using words that cultivate harmony such as, "Oh, I'm sorry this has happened to you." "I can really sympathize with you." "How may I help you?"

They Got Everything Wrong

One day I called a retail store to inquire about a product they special ordered for me. They had gotten it all wrong. Wrong size. Wrong model. Everything was wrong. I almost said, "You did not get one thing right with the order!" If I had said that, the clerk would have felt ridiculed. Instead of using Social Weapons, I refrained from casting blame. By avoiding the obvious attraction of being right, I kept myself from creating a big drama about something very small. The conversation remained cordial and when I finished reordering I really felt good. The clerk seemed to appreciate my courtesy. Had I decided to get some aggressive digs in, our interaction might have digressed into an ugly conflict.

Remaining Kind and Courteous is possible without losing touch with our issue. Trying to be too nice by giving up an issue can result in annoyance rather than defense of our boundaries. Making others' issues more important than our own issues can easily become a habit. Many of us choose the nice road to avoid conflict and forget that we need to be nice to ourselves, too. Remaining Kind and Courteous does not mean we have to fall into the trap of thinking, "I don't want to upset them so I'm just going to give up the whole thing," or "My needs are really not worth taking the chance of making them mad again."

Often, our tendency to be too nice stems from being afraid that others will not like us if we defend our territory. The trouble with being a martyr is that the martyr usually ends up bereft or hostile.

Being nice is like fighting with one hand hanging on to your halo while the other person is fighting with two hands.

Marianne K. Bakker-Rabdau

Chapter 32

SKILL # 6: THE WARRIOR'S STANCE

The Warrior's Stance refers to nonverbal behavior that helps us appear competent, fearless, and believable. What we are trying to convey with our visual image is that we are here to stay, well rooted into the ground, and not going anywhere until our issue is resolved. Our body language can demonstrate that we are focused, prepared, patient, confident, and have the inner fortitude to spend the time and effort needed to peacefully defend our territory. These qualities create a dynamic force that is the warrior's inner strength.

> *There are no contests in the Art of Peace.*
> *A true warrior is invincible because he or she*
> *contests with nothing. Defeat means to defeat*
> *the mind of contention that we harbor within.*
>
> **Morihei Ueshiba**
> *The Art of Peace*

Don Juan was a Yaqui Indian sorcerer, the central character in *Journey To Ixtlan* by Carlos Castaneda. In that book, Don Juan explained, "A warrior is not a leaf at the mercy of the wind. No one can push him; no one can make him do things against himself or against his better judgment." Don Juan emanated confident self-assurance by using the Warrior's Stance.

The physical image that we portray must be congruent with our verbal message. Giving someone a look of hatred when we call him our friend just does not work. Social science research strongly concludes that the majority of our communication is nonverbal.

The Warrior's Stance is a powerful skill for influencing other people. It also improves our performance when defending our territory. A calm fearlessness is demonstrated by standing tall. We pull our head back over our spine, pull our shoulders back, and lift our chests into an open position. We show our courage by leaning slightly toward the other person and maintaining eye contact. We demonstrate we are in no hurry by giving the impression that we could remain in the Warrior's Stance forever.

We can further display our mettle by keeping our speech calm, clear and firm. It works best by talking at a moderate pace, not too fast or too slow. After we have directly stated our issue, we need to remain silent. Using the Warrior's Stance will seem more powerful by avoiding the use of fillers, lead-ins, disclaimers, and apologies.

When combined with the skill Courtesy and the technique Creative Broken Record, the effectiveness of the Warrior's Stance can be exponentially enhanced. Combining skills and techniques that complement each other and best fit the situation create a powerful synergy.

The Warrior's Stance is not the same as being aggressively stubborn or pushy. When we behave that way we tend to use Social Weapons. These belligerent behaviors often come from feelings of entitlement or from the overwhelming need to be right. Maintaining the Warrior's Stance helps prevent us from behaving badly. Once we make a habit of conducting ourselves peacefully while consciously maintaining our stance, it is less likely that we will fall back on old habits of using Social Weapons. With continued practice, the Warrior's Stance becomes a new habit.

Chris Goes to the Prison

All of my practice using the Warrior's Stance paid off during my first experience in a state prison. Right after I finished graduate school, one of my professors asked me if I would teach a psychology class to inmate peer counselors at the state penitentiary. These counselors helped their fellow prisoners with adjustment problems. After I agreed to teach the class, my professor warned me that the prison guards would often try to harass anyone who came with the intent of "helping" the inmates. I soon found out what he meant.

Upon arriving at the prison, I checked in at administration and talked to the staff at the warden's office. They assured me that the guards had been notified and that I would be led to the prison's classroom without delay. Entry to the main prison building required standing between two sets of heavy steel bars with men possessing guns standing in cages on both sides. It was not a comfortable situation. I explained my business via a talk box, expecting to be let in immediately. Instead, I was told to wait.

I should mention that this happened back in the days following my military stint during the 1960's. In a relatively short period of time after being honorably discharged, my appearance had changed from a closely cropped soldier to a long-haired bearded graduate student. During the first five minutes I waited, three other people were allowed admittance through the double-barred entrance. I had a sinking feeling that I was in for a long wait.

It occurred to me that if I showed any sign of being upset the guards would make me wait each week. So, I opened my briefcase, took out a book, sat down and started to read. For the next 75 minutes I never looked up. This nonverbal behavior was used to appear as though I were content to sit there and read my life away.

When my name was called I didn't look up. I was projecting the image of not being in a hurry. My name was called again and I was told that I could go in. I cheerfully thanked the guard. For the next nine months I went to the prison every week. At each visit I gave and received a friendly greeting from the guards and was granted immediate entrance.

While using the Warrior's Stance, there are instances when it makes sense to modify our tone of voice and body language. When others won't look us in the eye, it may be that our eye contact is threatening. To help people feel more at ease we can use intermittent eye contact.

In the midst of telling people something they need to hear but do not want to hear, carefully gauge their reactions. If we see that they are being intimidated

or put off by our Warrior's Stance we have the option to adjust our look to fit the situation. Any modifications we make rely on our observation of the other party's responses. Our level of intensity can be constantly adjusted during the encounter. There are times when it makes sense to sit down or stand in a less imposing manner. Child protective service workers sometimes sit down to avoid creating a fight with an angry parent or guardian.

When we feel threatened by someone using Social Weapons, it's a signal for us to rethink our body language. Peaceful resolution is more likely to occur when we project our image in a way that encourages cooperation. We can do this with a Warrior's Stance that demonstrates we are calm, friendly, and not in a hurry.

Chapter 33

SKILL # 7: PLANNING STRATEGY

When our territory is invaded, we sometimes have to react immediately. More often we have time to plan how, when, and where we will use our Peaceful Self Defense System. Our attention to timing, choice of location, and style of confrontation will affect the outcome.

Timing is an important consideration to take into account when strategizing. The easiest time to defend our territory is right at the moment we experience irritation. This is because our reactionary emotions have not yet built up to full force, and the other has not had time to gain squatter's rights. By focusing on our issue, we are able to remain clear enough to avoid the pull of engaging in hostile behavior. Timing is an important part of our strategy as it allows us to avoid letting our emotions get the best of us.

Early defense of our boundaries can discourage the other party from invading further, gaining squatter's rights, or defining the incident as over and done with. Despite this, we may choose to postpone the confrontation for several reasons. We may wish to avoid an audience. We may wish to wait until we are in a better setting. We may be too tired or too emotional. My wife and I have an agreement not to bring up anything potentially upsetting near bedtime.

When Planning Strategy, think about where and when you will talk to the other person. On whose territory do we want to conduct the conversation? We are usually strongest on our home ground. On the other hand when dealing with insecure individuals, it can be good strategy to converse in a more neutral location where we are not perceived as being in an unfair or dominant position.

How do we want to defend? Do we want to do it alone or do we want to form an alliance? There is power in numbers. In college I was given what I thought was an unreasonable assignment. I gathered the class together and everyone said to the professor, "We'll take an 'F' in the course rather than do this assignment." The professor backed down. On my own, I probably would have flunked.

Face-to-face encounters are the most difficult yet also the most satisfying. The advantage of using the phone is we can use scripts or notes. Although the visual power of the Warrior's Stance is hidden from the listener on the phone, we can still take the posture and tone of the Warrior's Stance to boost our confidence.

If we we decide to choose the strategy of writing a letter we are providing all parties documentation of our issue. This strategy allows us to take our time, get help from others and include all the important details that need to be addressed. In business deals, letters are an important component of reaching an agreement.

Our appearance can be considered part of our strategy. By dressing well we create an image that causes others to react more favorably to us. A couple of my friends always dress up when they go shopping for clothes. One of them said to me, "You would be amazed at the difference this makes in the service we get."

When our clothes do not fit the situation we run the risk of not being recognized as equals. There is a fine line between a strategy that incorporates dressing well and using the Social Weapon *dress*. People are using the Social Weapon *dress* if their clothes cause a socio-economic hierarchy between them and others.

Audience effect can be powerful during conflict. When people are observing a conflict the nature of the interaction can be influenced by our tendency to play to the audience. Giving feedback in private is usually better accepted than doing it in public. Publicly advising people to change their behavior is more likely to be taken as a personal attack than as constructive criticism. Humiliating others in public creates friction and hostility. In some marriages there is an understanding that arguing under the public eye is taboo. The best strategy is to praise in public and criticize in private.

Sometimes the best strategy is to send an emissary such as a lawyer or friend who is better equipped to deal with the situation. In the case of a physical threat, as in the example of bullying that follows, it might be better to let the police be our emissary.

The Towel Snappers

Johnny's family moved from New Jersey to Oregon during the spring. Johnny was a freshman in high school. He soon found himself being targeted by the school bullies. He was constantly being tripped and made fun of. Johnny was on the receiving end of a towel snap just as the football coach was walking by. The coach yelled at them saying, "Hey, you two. Quit horsing around. One week in lunch detention for both of you!" During detention, the kid who was snapping the towel blamed Johnny for their punishment. The bully told Johnny, "You're going to pay for this!"

A week after Johnny was threatened, Johnny got undressed after gym class to take a shower. All at once, he found himself surrounded by a group of older kids wielding rolled up towels. Naked and out numbered, he received a severe beating. He was snapped by towels and kicked until the class bell rang. He had a welt under his eye and bruises around his private parts. At dinner, his parents asked him if he had been in a fight. They continued questioning him until he told them exactly what happened. The parents instantly employed the strategy of taking their battered child to the police station and filed assault charges.

Bullies usually deny they are bullies. Many are mean cowards with no sense of integrity. When caught

238

and confronted by someone in authority they usually lie about their behavior and deny any wrongdoing. One strategy for dealing with bullies is to keep a journal. Document everything. Write down the date, time, what happened, who did it, and what was done. Rather than trying to deal directly with the bully, use the Peaceful Self Defense System skills to get what you want from the appropriate authorities. Do this immediately and do not stop until you are satisfied that everyone is safe. The faster a bully gets consequences the sooner he or she will disappear into the woodwork.

To sum up strategy planning: In any situation we have three options:

1) Change the situation. This requires practice with the entire Peaceful Self Defense system.

2) Change how we look at the situation. This requires use of skill #8, reframing.

3) Get out of or withdraw from the situation.

Chapter 34

SKILL #8: PAYING THE PRICE

Unfair as it may seem, we usually pay a price for defending our territory. If the territory is an important one for all parties involved, the price for defending it may be high. Understanding the price is useful in situations such as deciding when to have a baby, whether to take a vacation or save money, or deciding whether to accept a promotion that involves travel.

How To Do A Cost-Benefit Analysis

Keep in mind that anything we do in a given situation has consequences. We can weigh the consequences of the use of the Peaceful Self Defense System versus not taking action. A negative consequence is called a cost. A positive consequence is called a benefit.

Let's assume we have identified our issue. Now we can choose what to do based on the following four guidelines:

1. Decide the importance of the issue. We can use the scale of 0-10 from the irritation log. The issue is likely more important to us if we are strongly irritated.

The more important the issue is, the more reason to decide whether to defend. Quantifying our irritation helps us determine the importance of an issue. If we are having a strong emotional reaction to it, chances are it is important.

2. Determine whether the issue comes up repeatedly. If it does, it is probably worth doing something about. This holds true even if the issue seems relatively unimportant. Small but daily irritations take their toll.

3. Make a chart listing our best predictions of what will happen if we fail to peacefully defend. Here are some common costs and benefits of not defending territory.

COSTS	BENEFITS
We may be angry or irritated with our self.	We will avoid unpleasant emotions.
We may lose territory.	We will temporarily avoid conflict.
We may feel irritation and anger toward the invader.	We have time to do other things.

4. Make a chart of what will happen if we do peacefully defend. Here are some common costs and benefits:

COSTS	BENEFITS
We may feel guilty for not doing what the other person wants.	We will be more likely to get what we want.
We may have to spend extra time defending.	We will start to establish a reputation for defending.
The other person may get mad at us.	We may gain respect from others.
The other person may not like us.	Our self-esteem will improve.
We may feel anxious or afraid.	We will have the chance to practice peaceful self-defense.

In summary, the best question to ask ourselves is, "What action will make me feel the best about myself?" When we fail to peacefully defend our territory the cost usually comes in the form of hostility. When we successfully defend our territory using the Peaceful Self Defense System our benefit comes in the form of peace.

What if someone is pressuring us for a prompt response? Remember, we can always ask for more time to think.

Chapter 35

SKILL #9: HANDLING NEGATIVE EMOTIONS

Reframing

Reframing is a way of viewing and experiencing events, ideas, and emotions to find more positive alternatives. How we feel about a situation controls how we think, feel, and behave. While one person may love parties, another may avoid them. One person may gravitate toward tough problems while another shuns them. Everything can be seen in more than one light.

Reframing often seems counter-intuitive. Solving the nine dot problem on the next page is an easy way to understand the skill of reframing. The challenge is to connect all nine dots with four straight lines by never lifting your writing instrument from the paper. Most people stay within the box bordered by the outer dots, when no actual box exists. The key to solving the problem is to venture outside the box.

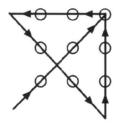

A Trip to The Space Needle

I can't remember where I read the article, but I remember the story it told. The tale was about a wife who was so hostile about picking up her husband's clothes that she had an emotional meltdown. She looked at his clothes all over the floor, went to the garage, found a hammer and a box of roofing nails. The wife then proceeded to nail every article of clothing to the spot where she found it. Pants and shirts were nailed to the coffee table. Socks and underwear were nailed to the floor. The man's sloth was off the chart so the project of nailing clothes ran through the entire house.

Some years after reading the article, I found myself working for Dr. Cornelis Bakker. He had trained my friend Charlotte and me in the Masters and Johnson's clinical approach to sex therapy. One day we were assigned to work with a couple who appeared to just hate each other. The husband was named Gunter and his wife was named Betsy. Gunter's complaint was that Betsy never stopped nagging and picking him apart. One of Betsy's many complaints was weariness from Gunter's failure to pick up his clothes. I had to restrain myself from asking, "Have you ever considered getting a hammer and a box of roofing nails?"

In addition to treating this battling couple with our regular protocol for sexual dysfunction, we had them play a game titled, "A Trip to the Space Needle." Betsy had always wanted to go to dinner at the Space Needle. Gunter told us he would not take her because it was too expensive. Betsy chimed in, "You see what a cheapskate he is?"

After hearing their comments, Charlotte and I devised a plan. We sketched a crude drawing on a piece of paper. During that time the couple continued to argue. I interrupted them by saying, "We have an idea that might set the stage for solving your sexual problems." Betsy looked at us and said, "You mean separating us by a thousand miles?" Charlotte smiled and said, "That might work, but that is not what we have in mind. We have devised a plan in the form of a game that you both might find agreeable."

I explained the game to the couple by saying, "The game is called *A Trip To The Space Needle*. It is played as follows: Every time Betsy picks up an article of Gunter's clothing, she gets to put a marker on the game board to advance one space closer to the top of the

Space Needle. Anytime Betsy complains to Gunter about leaving his clothes on the floor the marker goes back one space. When Betsy picks up enough clothing to reach the final square, Gunter has to take her to dinner at the Space Needle.

After two weeks of playing the game, the couple met with us. The marker was a couple of spaces short of reaching the final space on the game board. Betsy looked mad and sat down in a huff. Charlotte asked, "What's wrong?" Betsy replied, "The son-of-a-bitch is now picking up all his clothes!" Gunter added, "Well, she stopped nagging so I had to do something to keep her from winning." All four of us broke up in laughter. Behavior change can happen quickly when we learn to reframe how we look at problems. The experiment's outcome was that the couple began to enjoy each other's company.

Dr. Bakker studied the reasons why people don't change. He explained that the situations in which people find themselves control their behavior. Most of us believe that change is difficult and cannot be accomplished quickly. An effective way to change behavior is to change our situation. This modification becomes easier when the setting we are in facilitates our desired behavioral change. For instance, it would be counterproductive to spend our idle time in a bar if we are trying to quit drinking.

The IRS Auditor

Reframing can be an effective solution for dealing with a person of authority. Sadly, some bosses enjoy wielding power over their subordinates.

Pat was employed by the IRS. She came to me for counseling because she was in danger of being fired. Ken was her immediate supervisor. He seemed to need someone to pick on and Pat was his current target. During our counseling session, Pat was given the task of trying to reframe her response to Ken's provoking behavior. Every time he began to pick on Pat she was to express gratitude for his instruction and to express appreciation for the special attention she was receiving. I emphasized that if she was going to make this approach work she needed to project genuine humility.

My client was excited to put the plan to work. Every time Ken started to micromanage Pat, she would smile and softly say something like, "Thank you for taking the time to teach me a better way to do this." Ken was no longer stimulated by spending his time with Pat. He could see that his comments did nothing to make her uncomfortable. In less than a week Ken chose a new target to badger.

By projecting ourselves as being non-aggressive and humble, we increase the likelihood of reducing animosity. Taking away the expected reactive response and replacing it with humility and kindness reframes the way other people see us. Appearing unfazed can help us deal with people who are trying to enhance their status, or who feel compelled to be stimulated by knocking us down a peg or two.

Lazy Teenager

When someone uses the Social Weapon *withdrawal* it can easily provoke us to become upset and make us feel we have become the aggressive party. A common reaction is to tell the person using the Social Weapon how it makes us feel and this usually backfires. Any criticism or energy spent trying to get the other party to communicate demonstrates that their Social Weapon is working.

I worked with a client who had a teenage son. The young man used *withdrawal* on his mother every time she asked him to do his chores. The picture that was being framed was the mother nagging the boy about what she wanted him to do. I asked my client if she would like to try reframing rather than nagging. "What's reframing?" she asked. I explained the concept and went on to explain how quickly we could have a role reversal. I bet her that within three days her son would be nagging her.

The mother replied, "How can that be?" I continued, "Stop doing everything for him. Let him do it himself." She quickly inserted, "But, the place will be a mess. I won't be able to stand it." My reply was, "That is the price you will have to pay to change your situation."

The mother decided to take a chance. She was fed up with dealing with her kid. This time it was going to be her son doing the nagging.

The mother began taking back the territory she had been giving away for free. She stopped preparing meals. She stopped and ate at a cafe on the way home from work. She did none of his dishes and within two days the kitchen was a disaster. I told her in advance, "Don't worry, soon he will run out of food and there will be no need for dishes." She quit doing his laundry. She stopped cleaning up after him. Both mom and her son were seeing a new picture being framed.

As predicted, by the third day the son began to nag his mother about what her responsibilities were. He very quickly changed from the no fight strategy of *withdrawal* to using the Social Weapon *guilt*. The mother said, "When he began to nag me and try to make me feel guilty, I just laughed and felt totally under control." She reported that her son became eager to negotiate with her about what was expected of him.

To deal with the Social Weapon *withdrawal*, we need ask only one question: What am I giving the other person for free? *Withdrawal* is used to maintain the status quo. When we stop giving away desired territory, we can change the way an undesirable situation is framed. When the new picture points to higher priorities *withdrawal* tends lose it power. Those who use this weapon must change their course by speaking up in an effort to regain control. In so doing the Social Weapon *withdrawal* is neutralized.

Teaching Doctors To Be Courteous

Back when I was employed as an organizational development specialist I was given an assignment to teach all the doctors in a major medical center how to be more courteous. I thought to myself how this assignment might play out. At first I thought, "This is not going to be easy!" as I envisioned myself falling flat on my face trying to tell the chief of neurosurgery he needed to be more courteous. Eventually, I chose to reframe my negative thoughts to a picture that might appeal to the doctors.

The new picture was one of teaching the doctors how to handle difficult patients. The doctors had little trouble looking at a picture of difficult patients. Knowing the training was mandatory, I anticipated that the training was going to be met with some resistance. I assumed the doctors might say, "We don't have time for this! It is a waste of time -- we need to be seeing patients!" They would be using the Social Weapons *helplessness, ridicule* and *definition*. When the memo went out for the training, it was framed that learning the skills would save the M.D.'s time in their medical practice. It worked. In fact, it became so successful that I was later assigned to develop a model that is still used today.

When we fail to defend territory that is important to us our actions tend to become hostile. Reframing is a powerful tool that helps us avoid negative emotions and retaliatory behavior.

Facing Insults

The Social Weapon *ridicule* tends to trigger our negative emotions. Knowing how to combat *ridicule* can help us keep our cool, maintain control, stay on our issue, and experience a sense of satisfaction.

Facing *ridicule* is annoying. A rude comment, a disapproving glance, or downright slander can provoke us to become flustered. *Ridicule* is especially effective if it happens at a time when there is an audience or anytime we are taking ourselves entirely too seriously. People who use *ridicule* usually continue their onslaught until they are satisfied that their target is adequately perturbed.

To avoid becoming emotionally hooked by *ridicule* it is helpful to practice responses in advance. Taking *ridicule* on as an issue and using Creative Broken Record can help us stay above the fray. This is because we are better able to stay calm and confident when we know what to do. Using the skills helps us train the other party that there is no pay off for ridiculing us.

Ridicule is a powerful manipulation tool because its victims usually become discombobulated. *Ridicule* creates confusion by presenting two new issues at once. One issue consists of the way we are being insulted. The other issue consists of the content of the insult. This presents us with the choice of deciding which issue we should tackle first. By trying to cover both issues at once we can easily lose our composure and confidence.

Taking Ridicule On As An Issue

To take on *ridicule* as an issue, we simply tell the other person in an unfazed manner we do not like being ridiculed. As soon as we begin to defend against *ridicule* we can expect to be ridiculed again. Creative Broken Record is used to train a offender to stop ridiculing us by robbing him of stimulation. This is done by using Creative Broken Record as we calmly eat up his time until the *ridicule* stops.

Fred and Margaret

While taking the Peaceful Self Defense System class, Margaret realized her entire marriage had been held together only by her ability to put up with her husband Fred's constant abusive *ridicule*. She told me, "When I complain about his put downs the response is always the same, 'I'm just teasing, you are so thin skinned.' Or, 'You are just overly sensitive.'" Margaret continued, "You know Chris, it is just like you said. Every time I responded to the Social Weapon *ridicule* I get more *ridicule*."

When we can stick to an issue while appearing unaffected by another's *ridicule*, we rob them of the stimulation they get in continuing to *ridicule* us. Talking about how being ridiculed makes us feel usually invites more *ridicule*. Margaret asked me, "Don't you think my husband should respect my feelings." I answered, "Of course I do, but if you share your feelings with him when taking *ridicule* on as an issue it will usually lead to more *ridicule*. You might try letting him know what you want without revealing how he makes you feel. It might seem counter intuitive, but that is what seems to work."

After going home and being promptly ridiculed, Margaret seized the opportunity to practice Sticking to the Issue when Fred said, "I see the brainless wonder has arrived." Margaret, showing no emotion replied, "Fred, I don't like being ridiculed." Fred laughed and said, "I call them as I see them." Margaret continued to show no signs of succumbing to Fred's attack as she replied, "I realize you always call them as you see them and I still do not like being ridiculed."

Fred frowned and said, "After spending so much money and time on self improvement classes I'd think you could put up with a friendly tease now and then. You are always off doing things with others instead of with me." Without any hesitation Margaret said, "I

254

know you wanted me home today. You were very clear about that and I would really appreciate it if you stop your teasing." Fred replied, "Margaret, I don't mean anything by it. It's the way I talk." Margaret lovingly put her hand on Fred's shoulder and said, "Yes honey, I realize it is the way you talk and I would really appreciate it if you stopped teasing me." Fred finally got the point and said, "Okay, I'll try not to joke around so much."

Once Fred accepted Margaret's issue, she backed off from restating it. This example illustrates when to stop using Creative Broken Record. Margaret stopped after the issue of being ridiculed was acknowledged. When we ask for too many concessions it usually backfires. We cannot expect the offender to apologize because, in order to save face, people generally do not admit their transgressions.

Ignoring Ridicule

An effective way of handling the negative emotions that come with ridicule is to ignore any insults and go right on with our conversation or activity. This method works well to show offenders that their insults are ineffective. They are either going to ramp up the insults or give up trying. There's a good chance the insults will stop. However, if they persist, we can always turn to another strategy.

Ridicule Problem Solving

We can indicate a sincere desire to know what we did that the other person did not like. This is a useful technique if we think there is some truth to the *ridicule* and if the relationship is important. Let's say Tom called our statement about funding special education dumb. We could reply in a friendly tone of voice, "Tom, just what was it that you thought about it that was dumb?" If Tom continues to play his game, he might *ridicule* us again by saying, "If you don't know I can't explain it to you." In this case we might repeat our issue. "Just what was it that I said that you thought was so dumb?"

Sometimes finding the specifics behind the *ridicule* leads the conversation to constructive criticism that is helpful to both parties. This technique works very well when someone in authority puts us down. If our boss tells us we have been getting sloppy lately, we might stifle our defensiveness and take the opportunity to find out if he means our work, appearance, or both.

Doing It Up Right

Doing it up right is a technique that can be fun to employ. Running the *ridicule* into the ground becomes our basic strategy, as the following example illustrates:

Mean Mark tells Sally that she is stupid. Sally replies, "Yes, I am stupid. In fact, I come from a long line of people with low intelligence. My parents were certified dummies. Uncle Ralph, of whom we are all proud, has the record for the highest IQ in the family. He has an IQ of 16." This usually puts an end to someone trying to attack our egos.

It is difficult to *ridicule* someone who does not appear to take himself seriously. In the unlikely event others resume their insults, we can always say something like, "I wish I were as perceptive as some people. I am 100% stupid. Stupid is probably all I'll ever be." This technique works best if we let ourselves have a good time exaggerating how we fit the insults. A cheerful tone of voice and non-threatening body language and facial expressions work well to keep us from escalating conflict. The *ridicule* usually stops when the person hurling the insults sees us enjoying the exchange.

Giving A Snappy Answer

As we've seen, there are a number of peaceful ways to deal with the emotions that are triggered by *ridicule*. When we are being insulted, demeaned or belittled in front of an audience, the best defense might come in the form of a not so peaceful snappy answer. This answer usually includes the clever use of Social Weapons. Most of us are not ready with good snappy answers. When we do think of one it's usually too late.

*Repartee is something we think of
twenty four hours too late.*

Mark Twain

Who Do You Think You Are?

Many years ago I heard a good snappy answer while watching a TV show with my friend Charlotte. An actress on the show Star Trek was criticizing Captain Kirk and finished by saying, "Who do you think you are by doing this?" Captain Kirk replied without hesitation, "Who do I have to be?" Charlotte and I had to wait two years for the opportunity to use this line. We were co-teaching a class on the subject of this book when a man in the group became upset and got up and challenged us. We introduced an idea that he found unsettling. I could hardly believe it when he ended his discourse by saying, "Who do you think you are to be teaching this?" On cue, like two jack-in-the-boxes, we popped up and said in unison, "Who do we have to be?" The man sat down, unable to reply.

A good snappy answer can bring an expedient end to *ridicule* and entertain an audience. This approach, however, does not always promote good feelings. We have to gauge the situation. Every now and then someone with a quick wit can throw a snappy answer right back in response to ours and leave us speechless or laughing.

Disraeli's Retort

Benjamin Disraeli, the great English parliamentarian of the nineteenth century, was in a heated debate with Henry Gladstone when he came up with a memorable snappy answer. As Disraeli was speaking in the House of Commons, his rival Henry Gladstone rose from his seat in a rage and shouted, "Sir, you will either die on the gallows or of syphilis!" Disraeli's comeback was, "Sir, that depends on whether I embrace your politics or your mistress."

Most of us are unable to improvise as quickly as Disraeli. Those of us with slower wits might try remembering snappy answers we hear or read about. Once we have practiced a good comeback line we can look forward to a chance to use it

Doing The Unexpected

By being prepared to tackle insults, we are more likely to confidently, and in a timely manner, perform difficult-to-predict counter-strikes. These unexpected responses are best practiced in advance for neutralizing future *ridicule*.

Sometimes people will make ridiculing remarks that they expect to be ignored. We can spoil their fun by not ignoring them.

The next time we feel someone has insulted us, we could say "thank you." This is a quick and easy way to stop *ridicule*, unless the person insulting us happens to be our boss, or someone else with power over us.

Slowpoke

The last time I was at the airport I had to wait in a long line to get through security. When my turn came to go through, two young men behind me must have thought I hesitated too long because one said, "Okay, let's hurry it up slowpoke." I immediately turned around and asked them if they would like to go ahead of me. One of them apologized and began berating his friend.

The New Director From Redwood City

I used an unexpected retort when I became the Director of Social Work for a neurosurgical group. At my first regional director's meeting I was aghast when Herb, the man sitting next to me, stood up and shouted to the group, "Who here is from Redwood City?" Everyone knew I was from Redwood City. Herb shook his finger menacingly and shouted again, "Who here is from Redwood City?" I put my hand up and stated that I was. He then accused me, before the entire group, of making errors that he claimed inconvenienced his facility. Herb continued his tirade for several minutes and finished with a flourish as he shouted that my staff at

260

Redwood City never did anything right. Everyone present quietly watched, feeling relieved, I think, that he was yelling at me and not at them.

When Herb finished all eyes were on me. I deliberately paused before speaking. Looking at him directly, I confidently stated, "Being forced to observe your loud attention-seeking behavior, I would professionally diagnose you with histrionic personality disorder triggered by a dysfunctional sexual condition." Herb tried to speak, but no words came out. Everyone in the room broke into laughter as he sank back down into his seat. Later, I found out that he had earned a reputation for being an intimidating tyrant.

Looking back, I realize I attacked Herb using the Social Weapons *definition* and *ridicule*. I probably got away with my statement because everyone at the meeting was sick of Herb's unpleasant behavior. At the time I felt entirely justified for my retaliatory attack on Herb. Today, I genuinely regret not being kind and if I could do it over again I would use the Peaceful Self Defense System.

Herb continued being overbearing and intimidating to others but never again at my expense. Instead of responding to his accusations, I responded to his bullying public behavior. This was done by commenting on a very personal subject. Of course, I knew nothing of his sex life. However, by saying I did, it instantly ended his using *ridicule* on me.

When there is an audience and we are attacked with *ridicule*, the chances of conflict generally increase. Many times we are tempted to respond with Social Weapons, like I did with Herb, rather than employ Peaceful Self-defense System skills. If we use Social Weapons, it is important to be prepared for retaliation.

When I quieted Herb, I used Social Weapons to confuse him. I was fortunate Herb became so befuddled he was unable to escalate the conflict any further. To my surprise he was pleasant, respectful, and friendly to me during subsequent encounters.

The day after the encounter with Herb, my secretary informed me that Dorothy Kramer, a senior vice-president who sat in on the director's meeting, was waiting on the phone to speak to me. Before taking the call I told my secretary that I was probably about to be fired. I hesitantly picked up the phone and said, "Hello, Dr. Kramer." A friendly, almost laughing, voice said, "Hi, Chris. I am intrigued by the way you handled Herb yesterday. Did you operate off the cuff or was your approach something you can teach? I have been waiting for years to see someone shut that obnoxious man up."

This chapter has presented a variety of ways to handle negative emotions. In review, the methods include reframing, facing insults, taking ridicule on as an issue, ignoring ridicule, ridicule problem solving, doing it up right, giving a snappy answer, and doing the unexpected.

Chapter 36

SKILL #10: USING SELF-REINFORCEMENT

Research has shown that rewarding a given behavior increases the probability of that behavior being repeated. If we do something and it's rewarded, we are more likely to do it again. If we take a path that fails to reward us, we are less likely to make a habit of venturing along that same route.

Trespassers are not likely to encourage us to defend our boundaries. If a friend asks us if he can borrow our car and we refuse to give it to him, he is not likely going to praise us for our answer. Rarely will people thank us for limiting their encroachment into our territory. We have to reward ourselves. The reason we do this is to increase the probability that we will continue to protect our boundaries in the future.

Rewarding ourselves is important for promoting repetition of a given behavior. We may be doing something that we have never done before. We are taking a risk. It takes courage to defend our territory, especially in a difficult situation where the outcome is very important to us. Rewards and positive outcomes encourage us to continue putting in the time and effort needed to peacefully resolve conflict situations.

We call Using Self-Reinforcement a skill because it isn't something most of us do automatically. It's a skill like learning to write computer programs or using rules of etiquette. If we are like most people, we get down on ourselves for something we did wrong a lot faster than we reward ourselves for something we did right. If we utilize a Peaceful Self Defense System skill and are rewarded for it, chances are we will do it again.

There is always something we can use as a reward. We might make a deal with ourselves that after we successfully defend a boundary we buy ourselves something special. A more powerful reward can be the praise we get from friends for standing up for ourselves.

Earlier I described an episode of Sticking to the Issue while on foot at a drive-through bank window. As I was standing in the bank line I was thinking, "This is going to make a great story for class and my friends will get a kick out of it too." As we tell people about our adventures in communication, they might realize that they, too, can defend their boundaries.

Further rewards come from the development of our confidence and the gratification of successfully solving our problems. The old saying, "practice makes perfect," is true. The more we seize opportunities to practice communication skills the better equipped we become at solving more difficult problems.

Chapter 37

SKILL #11: PRACTICING DELAYED MASTERY

Since the mind is conditioned by the past,
you are then forced to reenact the past again
and again.

Eckhart Tolle
A New Earth

The problems presented to us in life continuously repeat themselves. Following a bad experience, we usually have time to create and practice a plan for dealing with similar events in the future. Practicing Delayed Mastery consists of a review of how we dealt with what occurred and then reconstructing the event as we wished we had handled it.

Practicing Delayed Mastery should be considered anytime our response to a negative encounter fails to satisfy us. A similar event will most likely occur again. It makes sense for us to prepare for what we are going to do so we can be confident and composed the next time it happens.

Through mental rehearsal we can fine tune our responses in order to counter or diminish the impact of similar attacks. It is helpful for us to think in a positive manner by visualizing being successful as we practice for upcoming encounters. Sometimes we are forewarned of challenges that we have never experienced before. We would do well to plan and practice for these events ahead of time. Being prepared, we have our pre-practiced defense instantly at hand rather than something we think of after the fact.

Athletic Performance

The skill of Practicing Delayed Mastery is a performance booster practiced by athletes. In 1968, the defending world cup champion Jean-Claude Killy went to the Olympics and won gold medals in all three alpine skiing events. Killy, prior to an important competition, would imagine skiing down a slope 500 times. In his mind he saw the contours of the slope, felt his body moving in perfect control, and felt his winning speed. Golfers, tennis players, martial artists, and other athletes also practice in their minds to improve their performance.

Called behavioral rehearsal, or creative reverie, this technique can be used to replay and improve upon our ability to perform well in defending our territory. This does not mean beating ourselves up for our mistakes. It is focused on rehearsing our future actions for a similar problem.

Reverie is a short, consciously-guided thought process where we can direct and change our approach for dealing with a situation. Reverie is an aid for looking at ourselves objectively. This practice helps us assume an attitude of non-attachment. When we remember an event that we judge to be a negative occurrence, we have the option to stop the film strip of thought at any frame. We can study a frozen moment in time in an effort to figure out how to manage these situations in the future.

Extreme Climber Alex Honnold

Most experts in the world of rock climbing concede that extreme free solo climber Alex Honnold is the best climber alive today. He climbs rock walls higher than the Empire State Building. He climbs solo with no ropes, no protection, and no help. It is just the wall, the elements, and him. The only gear he uses is a bag of chalk and rubber climbing shoes. In 2011, Alex became the first person to free solo the Sentinel, a rock face of Half Dome in Yosemite National Park. This sheer face is 1600 feet straight up. No climbers had ever attempted such a dangerous feat. The mind boggling ascent took Alex just under ninety minutes to complete.

Combat Reporter Lara Logan, who spent years in Iraq and Afghanistan, was covering Alex's riveting climb. After the climb was completed, Lara, who has a reputation of remaining cool under fire, finally stopped holding her breath. Before the climb, Lara asked Alex if he felt any adrenaline. Alex replied, "There is no adrenaline rush, you know? Like, if I get a rush, it means that something has gone horribly wrong, you know? Because the whole thing should be pretty slow and controlled and like, I mean, it's mellow."

Alex told Lara that he visualized every foot hold and hand hold up the face of the climb in advance. This type of visualizing, rehearsing, and planning is creative reverie. Alex climbed the north face two times with ropes and gear to evaluate the terrain. He did not free climb the Sentinel cliff blindly. Before his feat, Alex repeatedly visualized climbing the face until he had the route mentally mastered. Largely because of this preparatory practice, Alex was able to remain confident enough to maintain an attitude of non-attachment and complete focus in the moment. There was no panic or emotional upheaval to distract and undermine his attention to detail.

Chapter 38

SKILL #12: SIGNALING DEFENSIVE INTENT

Most people are in the habit of using Social Weapons to accumulate more physical and psychological ownership. They use manipulation in order to get what they want and unconsciously or purposefully raid the territory of others. Unless we let them know that we will not tolerate their invasions, they will continue to chip away at our territorial boundaries.

Signaling Defensive Intent is a potent way to avoid having to defend territory. Clearly signaling our intent to defend territory can make it unnecessary to use the rest of our defense system. Signaling can be in the form of written words, facial expressions and body language, or verbal statements. By warning people in advance of our resistance to encroachment, we will be less likely to experience attacks. Signaling Defensive Intent can take the form of posting signs, fencing off an area, or providing employees with a handbook that contains company expectations, policies and procedures.

To be left alone by family members at home we might tell them that we are tired, need to take a nap, and would appreciate not being disturbed. When discussing a dinner engagement with friends we can warn them in advance that we are going to leave promptly at a certain time. When we anticipate an unwanted encroachment into our territory, we usually have the option of presenting a clear picture of our boundaries and what we are willing to do to preserve them. Simple pre-emptive warnings can help us avoid having to pay the price of dealing with unwanted trespasses.

Haridas Chaudhuri is considered a master of Integral Psychology. In his book, *Mastering the Problems of Living* he gives an account of an ancient Hindu story that illustrates the importance of Signaling Defensive Intent. His story is about a large serpent that was terrorizing a village. One day a holy man was passing through the village. He was told about the misdeeds of the serpent. The holy man found the serpent and convinced it to live a more peaceful life. The serpent became so passive that the village children began hitting it with objects until it went into hiding to die. After a few days the holy man returned to the village and found the dying serpent. The serpent complained that the holy man's advice was going to get him killed. The holy man said, "I told you not to bite any living creature. But why did you not hiss when you were attacked?"

> *Love has to be protected with the voice of thunder.*
>
> **Haridas Chaudhuri**
> ***Mastering the Problems of Living***

When we feel our territory is being invaded, it is advisable to give off a warning display. It might come in a human equivalent of a snake hiss. It could be a glare, a show of force or a statement that strongly advises an aggressive retaliation is imminent if the transgressor fails to retreat.

The Paradox of the Peaceful Self Defense System

The Peaceful Self Defense System helps us develop the confidence to defend, and sends a message to others that we are not easy victims. Fewer attempts of trespass into our territory occur when we unhesitatingly signal our message of willingness to defend. The Peaceful Self Defense System paradox is that the better we get at defending, the less we have to defend. We can expect fewer challenges when we are fully prepared and ready to take action. Trespassers tend to leave us alone as we become more proficient at dealing with them. When we are in a state of readiness and show an appearance of confidence, we often experience others retreating before we have to give off more intimidating warning signals. The appearance of being able to successfully defend our territory often becomes our best defense.

Alex the Cat

I had a cat named Alex. For many years any cat that crossed his territory was met with a severe beating. Alex lived for over twenty-three years. That is a long life for a cat. The other cats in the neighborhood went out of their way to avoid him, as he was able to exude a confidence that kept his self-defense paradox in place. The last three years of his life Alex had trouble just walking and most other cats could have easily won a fight with him, but none tried. Alex had developed an air of confidence that other cats could sense. He projected an image that made physically defending his territory unnecessary. A fearless appearance kept Alex from being attacked.

Small Issues Help Form Our Reputation

Practicing the skills with small unimportant issues can be key to building our reputation. Remaining on the phone with an uninvited solicitor is a safe way to hone our skills when our only sacrifice is the time we are willing to spend. When we know what to do, we can relish the opportunity to assume the Warrior's Stance, Remaining Kind and Courteous while practicing Creative Broken Record on relatively mundane issues.

We do not create our reputation by winning one big battle. We create our reputation by adequately defending against the day in and day out routine issues of life. Not only do other people begin to respect us when we say 'no', often they sanction themselves and avoid even trying to intrude into our space.

Consistency Stops Intrusion

Effectively defending a territory requires consistency. We can expect others to regularly attempt to cross our boundaries if we fail to be persistent in guarding what we want to maintain. The vital point that most people ignore is that intrusion grows greater when it does not meet opposition.

Persistence gives confidence, and continued right mental attitude followed by consistent action will bring success.

Claude M. Bristol
The Magic of Believing

Adequately defending a boundary does not always put an end to people trying to trespass again. If we are vigilant and consistently defend our territory, after a few attempts our reputation will begin to defend for us. Habitual trespassers usually ignore warning signs. Once they discover that we back up our warnings they are less likely to cross our boundaries.

Be Someone Else

If we fear punishment for standing up to another person, we might want to pretend that we are someone else. Rather than getting upset we can pretend that we are someone who does not easily get pushed around. Let us pretend we are Mahatma Gandhi, Clint Eastwood or Gloria Steinem. We might consider what they would do if they were being denied what they needed. Then we role play how they might implement the Peaceful Self Defense System to fit their respective personalities.

Self-Fulfilling Prophesies

It benefits us to be keenly aware of the consequences of creating self-fulfilling prophesies. Whether we think we can or think we can't, we usually end up being right. This is a case of what we believe becoming reality. Optimistic confidence has a big effect on success. The odds of being successful increase once we have faith in our ability to defend our territory.

There will be times when we fail to be considerate to others and mistakenly think we are following the Peaceful Self Defense System. Catching our own use of Social Weapons is necessary to navigate this dynamic operating system. To live more peacefully we would do well to continually monitor how our behavior affects the behavior of those around us. In order to stay on a solid path to peace we must continue to use peaceful skills and consciously refrain from fighting with Social Weapons.

The Dalai Lama's Rule

There are situations when we think we don't have the time and energy needed for peacefully dealing with unreasonable people. When faced with irrational and unkind people we might catch ourselves feeling justified to fight back using Social Weapons. Retaliating with Social Weapons usually leads to intensifying the battle. Resorting to any kind of weapon use is like pouring gas on a fire. Social Weapon use can be thought of as building bad karma because harm that goes around often comes back around. Harming anyone breaks the Dalai Lama's rule of being kind whenever possible. He maintains that it is always possible to be kind.

The more we study and practice the Peaceful Self Defense skills, the more likely it is that we'll be able to successfully defend our boundaries. Like an accomplished martial artist whose reputation discourages others from attacking, mastering self-defense skills and strategies can discourage further attacks. Those of us who regularly practice these peaceful techniques are laying down a strong foundation of behavioral habits that will help us form better relationships.

CONCLUSION

Social Weapons are to humans what water is to fish. Water is the medium in which fish exist. The medium in which we exist is so fraught with Social Weapons that their use is as invisible to us as water is to a fish. We take them for granted and see them as normal human expression. Social Weapons are ingrained in our social interactions and we usually are unaware of the competitive influence they exert over us. Humans are territorial animals. We tend to fight over our boundaries with Social Weapons. A territorial perspective gives us the ability to make sense of what motivates people to attack others. This understanding helps us realize why our own behavior is sometimes out of control.

The Peaceful Self Defense System provides a universal approach for peacefully defending our territory. This approach can be adapted for use in most human conflicts. Being well practiced at fine tuning our use of the system can help prevent ordinary human relations from turning into scenes of in-your-face combat. When we use this system our underlying imperative is to protect our territory without creating more conflict. By understanding and seeing through the Social Weapons that trigger our emotions we are less likely to become hostile. As we become more proficient using the Peaceful Self Defense System it becomes easier to find ways to create peace.

Be grateful even for hardship, setbacks, and bad people. Dealing with such obstacles is an essential part of training in the Art of Peace.

Morihei Ueshiba
The Art Of Peace

Peacefully dealing with people when they use Social Weapons is made possible by consistent practice. Regular use of the peaceful skills helps increase our confidence and poise. This training develops our ability to remain kind, courteous, and focused in moments of conflict. Social Weapon attacks can be viewed as opportunities for defending our boundaries and practicing the skills. Monitoring our own use of Social Weapons is necessary for considerate behavior. In the process of defending our territory and the boundaries around it, we find opportunities to create peaceful resolutions. After enough practice we tend to see situations go our way as our lives become less adversarial and more pleasant.

The best way to learn the system is to share it with others. If we convince our family and friends to embrace the Peaceful Self Defense System, we help create a kinder community around us. Our goal is to create many of these communities and make the world a more peaceful place.

ABOUT THE AUTHORS

Chris Storey

Chris has a Master's Degree in Social Work from the University of Washington. He has worked for hospitals as an organizational development specialist, director of social work and cognitive behavioral therapist. He also maintained private clinics and hosted a radio program. Chris has been teaching and refining the Peaceful Self Defense System for over four decades. His work draws on insights from teaching his system to employees of major corporations, government organizations, civic groups and the students at numerous colleges and universities. Chris teaches with humor, wit and enthusiasm. His passion is ultra distance running with a personal record of 103 + miles in 24 hours.

Doug Casey

Doug graduated from the University of Washington and has been a life long entrepreneur. He currently owns the Mystery Gallery, a rock shop, with his wife Kathy in Oak Grove, Oregon. Doug was a member of the Somali 1988 and 1992 Olympic Medical Staff. Part of his life's work has been to help athletes achieve their goals.

The authors welcome comments and questions. E-mail: socialweapons@gmail.com.